PRIVATIZATION
Investing in State-Owned Enterprises Around the World

Also from Ernst & Young

The Ernst & Young Guide to Total Cost Management
The Complete Guide to Special Event Management
The Ernst & Young Guide to Raising Capital
The Ernst & Young Guide to Expanding in the Global Market
The Ernst & Young Resource Guide to Global Markets
Understanding and using Financial Data: An Ernst & Young
   Guide for Attorneys
The Ernst & Young Business Plan Guide, Second Edition
Managing Information Strategically
(*The Ernst & Young Information Management Series*)
Mergers & Acquisitions, Second Edition
The Ernst & Young Almanac and Guide to U.S. Business Cities
The Name of the Game: The Business of Sports
The Ernst & Young Guide to Financing for Growth

PRIVATIZATION
Investing in State-Owned Enterprises Around the World

Ernst & Young

JOHN WILEY & SONS, INC.

New York • Chichester • Brisbane • Toronto • Singapore

Library of Congress Cataloging in Publication Data:
Privatization : investing in infrastructures around the world / Ernst
  & Young.
     p.   cm.
  Includes bibliographical references.
  ISBN 0-471-59323-0
  1. Privatization. 2. Investments, Foreign. 3. Infrastructure
(Economics)--Finance. I. Ernst & Young.
HD3850.P747   1994
338.9--dc20   93-45615

Printed in United States of America

10 9 8 7 6 5 4 3 2 1

ACKNOWLEDGMENTS

The authors want to express their appreciation to those who helped in the preparation of this book. Nancy Ashken, Ernst & Young's Marketing Manager for International Services, was the source of the original inspiration for the book. Marian Gibbon and Holly Thorsen, of Ernst & Young's International Finance and Investment Consulting Services Group, contributed their research and editorial talents. Ernst & Young's Colombo, Sri Lanka office, also contributed valuable background materials. Mort Myerson, Ernst & Young's National Director of Public Communications, contributed valuable insights as well as his diplomatic talents when the inevitable differences of opinion arose between authors and editors. Finally, we wish to thank all of the business people who were so generous with their experiences investing in state-owned enterprises, which we feel contribute so much to the value of this book.

CONTENTS

INTRODUCTION

Privatization is an investor's guide to the current global privatization phenomenon. The conversion or sale of former state-owned enterprises (SOEs) to privately owned institutions is occurring on a scale that few could have predicted ten years ago. Over 10,000 SOEs in more than 100 countries have been sold to private interests in the past decade.

Other attractive opportunities are available to investors who can identify viable SOEs and negotiate a favorable deal for them. Privatization is designed to meet the needs of the prospective equity investor in SOEs rather than the portfolio investor. Its objective is to equip you with a general understanding of the privatization process and then to provide you with practical guidance at every step of the process by describing

- How to decide if SOEs in general offer the best opportunity for you to achieve your business objectives

- How to identify potentially attractive SOE investment opportunities and obtain additional information on them

- How to pick the SOE that offers the best opportunity

- How to navigate through the complexities of the privatization process and negotiate the best deal

- How to begin building your newly acquired asset into an effective company

- Where to go for professional advice and assistance

The information presented in this guide is practical and implementation oriented rather than theoretical. It should be sufficient to take the sophisticated or independent-minded investor, whether an individual or an institution, from A to Z in the privatization process. Nevertheless, it is impossible to deal exhaustively with all of the complexities and potential complications of the privatization process in a book such as this. We therefore strongly recommend that you consider obtaining professional assistance from one or more of the sources described in Chapter 11.

Before you begin to read this guide, take the time to ask yourself several questions:

- What are my overall financial and business objectives?

- What do I hope to accomplish by investing in an SOE (increased competitiveness in my existing markets, new products or technology, market access)? How do these objectives fit in with my overall financial and business strategy?

- What resources (financial, material, and human) am I prepared to put into this project?

- What is my time frame for initiating and completing this transaction?

The book is organized into two parts, consisting of a total of eleven chapters. Part I is a general introduction to privatization and consists of five chapters:

- Chapter 1, "Selling the State," provides a broad definition of privatization.
- Chapter 2, "Why Privatize?" is an analysis of governments' and other concerned parties' interests and objectives in privatization.
- Chapter 3, "Methods of Privatization," gives a comprehensive description—and the pros and cons—of the wide variety of privatization mechanisms that are available to governments and investors.
- Chapter 4, "Worldwide Experience in Privatization," relates the discussion in Chapters 1 through 3 to what has actually been happening in the world.
- Chapter 5, "The Making of a Successful Privatization Program," identifies the main reasons that some nations' privatization programs have been far more successful than others.

Part II is a practical guide to privatization for the investor. The emphasis in Part II is on providing specific advice on what do and how to go about doing it in order to maximize the chances of success. Five of Part II's chapters correspond roughly to the successive stages in the privatization process, beginning with the development of a strategic framework for the proposed investment, and continuing through the selection of an acquisition target and negotiation of a deal, to restructuring the newly acquired company.

Some readers, particularly those who already have an SOE in their investment sights, may prefer to skip ahead to the sections on due-diligence analysis and on carrying out the transaction. However, we recommend that you read from the beginning, because the book presents a consistent overall approach to privatization that is designed to maximize the investor's benefits.

- Chapter 6, "Should I Invest In an SOE?" addresses the advantages and risks that privatization offers the investor. Its objective is to enable the investor to determine if investing in an SOE is compatible with his or her overall business strategy, or whether an alternative approach would be preferable.

- Chapter 7, "What Country Should I Invest In?" discusses what makes some countries a more suitable environment for investing in an SOE than others. The first part of the chapter focuses on the general problem of deciding which countries offer the best investment prospects. The second part is a discussion of so-called country risks for the investor who has tentatively settled on a particular SOE.

- Chapter 8, "Choosing the Right Investment Target," describes a three-stage process for establishing a "short list" of potential SOE investment targets and then narrowing down the range of alternatives until a choice is reached.

- Chapter 9, "Negotiating a Deal," describes the way in which the privatization process actually works and gives investors some advice on how to use the process to secure the best terms.

- Chapter 10, "The Management Challenge," is written for the investor who has completed the privatization transaction. While a privatized SOE is like any other turnaround situation in some ways, it also has important differences that the investor should be aware of and factor into his or her strategy.

The final chapter in Part II, Chapter 11, "Getting Assistance," informs the reader about useful sources of information and assistance, particularly the potential role of such professional advisers as consultants, accountants, lawyers, and investment bankers in structuring a successful privatization project.

PART I

A General Introduction to Privatization

CHAPTER 1

"Selling the State"

Privatization is the great economic transformation process of our time. More than 10,000 state-owned enterprises (SOEs) in over 100 countries have been privatized, not including the literally hundreds of thousands of small shops, service businesses, and farms that have been taken over by private owners. Even the privatizers are going private: the Treuhand, the German government agency that has overseen the divestiture of East Germany's public sector, is now offering its services internationally as a paid privatization consultant. The Treuhand reportedly is currently seeking private investors.[1]

As a student of international economics, or perhaps even as an investor in a state-owned enterprise, you may want to deepen your understanding of this phenomenon that is sweeping the world. The first five chapters of this book are devoted to developing such an understanding of the privatization process, including its evolution around the world, and where it has been most successful and why. Chapter 6

---

[1]*Privatisation International* (April 1992), p. 7.

through 11, written especially with the investor in mind, contain a practical description of the steps involved in investing in an SOE.

A BROADER DEFINITION OF PRIVATIZATION

Privatization means more than the sale of ailing public companies at fire sale prices. "Privatization" can be defined broadly as the transfer or sale of any asset, organization, function, or activity from the public to the private sector. As such, in addition to the sale of publicly owned assets, the term "privatization" also applies to joint public-private ventures, concessions, leases, management contracts, as well as to some specialized instruments, such as build-own-operate-and-transfer (BOOT) agreements. (See Chapter 2 for a more detailed explanation of these terms.) Each of these approaches to privatization offers different opportunities to investors who are prepared to take advantage of them.

PRIVATIZATION AS A PROCESS

Privatization is more than an event; it is a process by which state-owned assets or activities are transferred to the private sector. Naturally, the details differ by country and by type of transaction, but the process for privatizing a typical state-owned enterprise, as depicted in Figure 1-1, is fairly representative.

The privatization process has three phases: (1) preparation, (2) privatization, and (3) postprivatization. In the first phase, preparation, selected enterprises or activities are first targeted for privatization, either as the outcome of a planning process or as a result of an investor's expression of interest. In the case of an SOE, the next step is typically "corporatization," in which the enterprise that has been

FIGURE 1-1   The privatization process

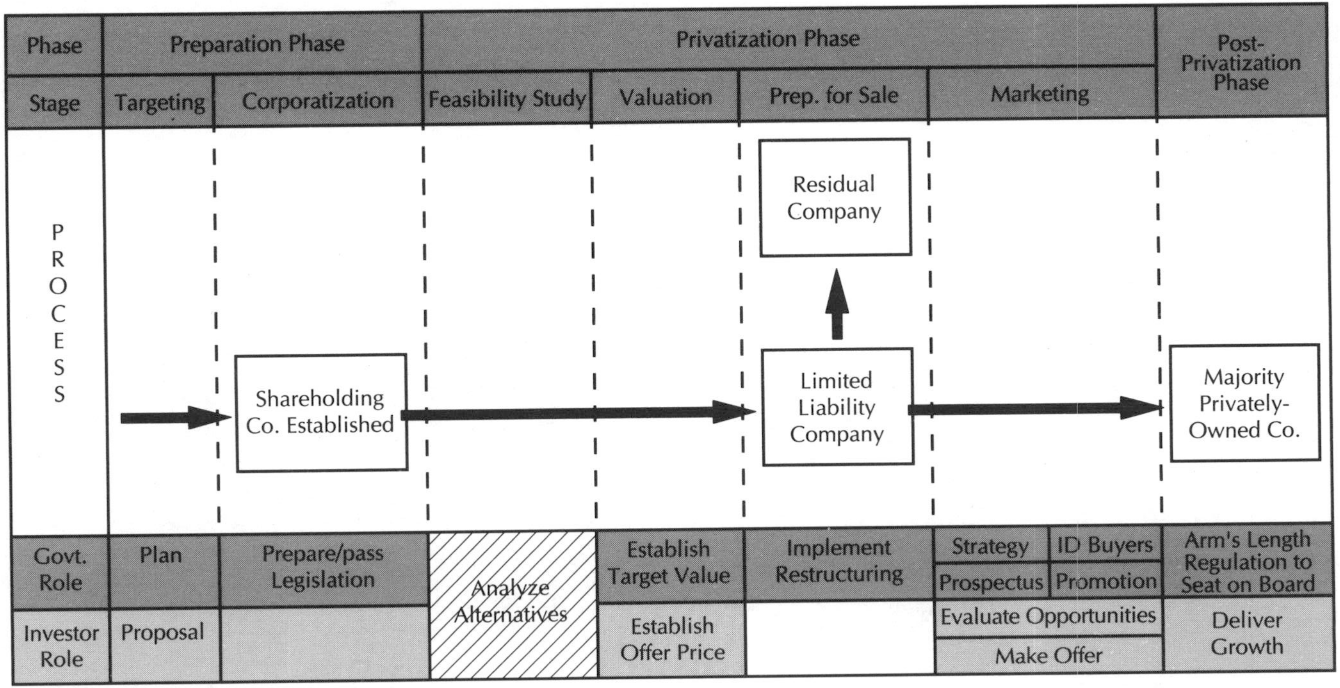

Phase	Preparation Phase		Privatization Phase					Post-Privatization Phase
Stage	Targeting	Corporatization	Feasibility Study	Valuation	Prep. for Sale	Marketing		
P R O C E S S		Shareholding Co. Established			Residual Company / Limited Liability Company		Majority Privately-Owned Co.	
Govt. Role	Plan	Prepare/pass Legislation	Analyze Alternatives	Establish Target Value	Implement Restructuring	Strategy / ID Buyers	Prospectus / Promotion	Arm's Length Regulation to Seat on Board
Investor Role	Proposal			Establish Offer Price		Evaluate Opportunities	Make Offer	Deliver Growth

Source: Ernst & Young, *The Global Sweep of Privatization* (London, Euromoney Publications PLC, 1990) pp. 6–7.

targeted for privatization is transformed into a sharehold-ing type of company, with the government holding 100 per-cent of the shares for the time being.

In the second phase, privatization, the government and its advisers undertake a study to assess the feasibility of privatiz-ing the enterprise or activity and the mechanisms available for achieving this objective. Projections of future revenues also are an important element in determining the govern-ment's asking price. In many cases, the interested investor will be performing parallel analyses of his or her own.

Depending on the conclusions reached in the strategic assessment, the government may decide to restructure the enterprise before putting it up for sale, in order to increase its marketability. For example, the government may hive off non-revenue-generating employee welfare activities, such as holiday resorts, "research institutes", or perennially loss-making plants.

Financial restructuring is also often part of the prescrip-tion. Many public enterprises are heavily indebted to state banks, and some form of loan forgiveness or debt-equity swap may be required in order to put the enterprise on a financial footing that is acceptable to investors.

The government's strategy for marketing the enterprise is influenced by the enterprise's strategic interests, legal provisions, and the political realities of the host country. In cases in which the government decides to market at least a portion of the shares to foreign investors, the government and its advisers (frequently an investment bank) target can-didate investors, prepare a prospectus or offering memo-randum, and try to drum up a sale.

In the third and final phase, postprivatization, the inves-tor takes over the operation of the enterprise. Most inves-tors undertake further restructuring, with an emphasis on improving the quality and reducing the cost of the goods or services provided. The government's role in the final, postprivatization phase may vary, from arm's-length regulation or a continuing involvement in the running of the enterprise, on the one hand, to seats on the board of directors for the government or its proxies (e.g., social insurance or pension funds), on the other hand.

THE "ENABLING ENVIRONMENT" FOR PRIVATIZATION

A still broader definition of "privatization" would have to include not only the mechanisms that are available to investors who wish to acquire shares in former state-owned enterprises, but also the process by which those mechanisms are implemented. Ths definition also would have to include all of the policy, legal, institutional, financial, infrastructural, and other elements that are prerequisites of a functioning market economy, without which private investments in those countries are likely to fail. We can call these elements the "enabling environment" for privatization.

The overall political and economic health of the host country are important aspects of the enabling environment, but other important aspects include the following:

- *Policy environment:* Liberalization of domestic and foreign trade, relaxation of price controls, balancing of the government's finances in order to reduce the public sector's demands for available financial resources.

- *Legal environment:* Furnishing the legal framework necessary to reassure private investors and to guarantee the orderly functioning of the market economy (e.g., laws on private property, enterprise law, contract law, laws on taxation).

- *Regulatory environment:* Providing the degree of oversight necessary to prevent misuse or abuse of the system (e.g., antimonopoly, banking, securities and exchange regulations), consistent with the government's reduced role in the economy.

- *Financial environment:* Affording investors and business-people access to sufficient capital to finance new investments, the expansion of existing facilities, and working capital requirements, through the banking system or financial markets.

- *Infrastructure:* Developing the energy, water, telecommunications, and transport facilities required for businesses to obtain needed goods and materials, to communicate with suppliers and customers, and to bring the final product to market quickly and efficiently.

- *Training and technical assistance:* Nurturing and developing the entrepreneurial and business management skills that may have atrophied during the years of public ownership of the means of production and centralized planning.

- *A social "safety net":* Cushioning the impact of the transition to a market economy on the weaker segments of the economy.

The importance of the policy aspects of the enabling environment should not be underestimated. The World Bank has collected data that show that the policy environment may have accounted for as much as one-third of the returns on a wide cross-section of private investment projects. In a relatively undistorted policy environment, the probability of a project being successful (i.e., with a rate of return of 10 percent or more) was more than twice as great as that of being successful in a high-distortion environment.[2]

---

[2] World Bank. *World Development Report, 1991: The Challenge of Development* (New York: Oxford University Press, 1991), pp. 70–87.

CHAPTER 2

Why Privatize?

Although the idea of privatization has been around for a long time (Adam Smith wrote about it as long ago as 1762), privatization has been tried widely only since the mid-1970s. Privatization first attracted worldwide attention in 1979 when the Conservative government of Prime Minister Margaret Thatcher began transforming the ailing U.K. economy by selling public holdings in industry, communications, and other service sector areas. Since 1979, over 100 countries have initiated their own privatization programs.

The reasons for privatization's newfound popularity vary among different countries and interest groups. It is important to remember that national governments are not the only parties with a stake in privatization. Other "stakeholders" include local government officials and the managers and workers of the SOEs being privatized. Even politicians, bureaucrats, and technocrats in the national government may be divided in their views (see Figure 2-1).

FIGURE 2-1   Privatization stakeholders

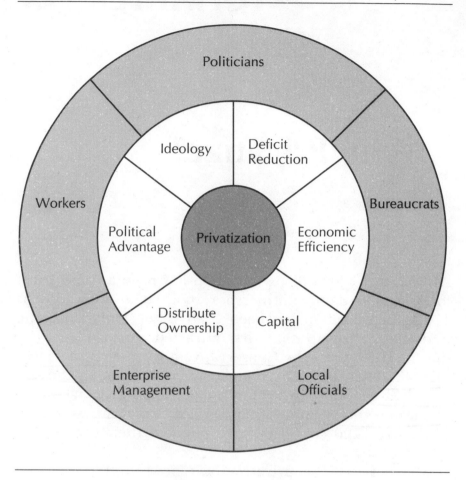

OBJECTIVES OF NATIONAL GOVERNMENTS

The interest of national governments, which includes elected politicians and appointed bureaucrats, may be ideological, pragmatic, or, more frequently, a combination of both. Pragmatic reasons for supporting privatization may be both political and economic.

Most of the ideological justifications for privatization reflect some variant of the belief that government has become too large, that the private sector can do many things more effectively and efficiently than the public sector, and that activities which are peripheral to the real business of running the country are diverting money and skilled personnel away from more important activities. Perhaps the outstanding example of a government with an overriding ideological commitment to privatization is the former British government of Prime Minister Margaret Thatcher, whose example arguably made a greater contribution to fostering the spread of privatization than any other government.

There has been an accelerating trend in most parts of the world—not only in Eastern Europe and the former Soviet Union, but also in Africa, Latin America, and Asia—toward the installation of democratically elected governments or at least governments that consider themselves to be more representative of the people's interest than the former totalitarian or authoritarian regimes.

A corollary of this development is that many of the new governments have sought to increase worker and/or popular participation in the ownership of national assets. A number of governments in Eastern Europe and the former Soviet Union have implemented or are discussing "mass privatization" programs, in which every citizen receives coupons, either free or at a nominal charge, that can be redeemed for shares in state-owned enterprises. Present and, in some cases, former employees of the SOE may be allowed to buy shares at a discount—a privilege that is also extended to former political prisoners in some countries.

The pragmatic arguments for privatization include both political and economic arguments, which of course are closely interrelated. Politicians naturally want to attract political support by increasing the general level of economic well-being, as well as by extending direct economic benefits to strategically placed members of the electorate (e.g., by allowing workers to buy shares in companies at a discount.) Reducing the size and importance of the public sector may further help the government to consolidate its position by depriving the potential opponents of its power base in state enterprises and the ministries or agencies that control them.

Privatization is also viewed by many officials as a way in which to jump-start many nations' stalled economies. The biggest economic success stories of the 1980s took place in countries whose economies gave the fullest play to the private sector, such as the United States, Germany, Japan, Korea, Taiwan, Hong Kong, and Singapore, providing a vivid contrast to the lackluster performance of most European "social democracies" and the downright dismal track record of most of the rest of the world, which generally followed the Socialist model of development.

The transition to democratically elected or at least more popular governments in many countries has helped to unleash a tide of rising expectations for a better life among their populations. To meet these expectations, particularly during a period in which many foreign aid donors' budgets are pinched or stretched thin, these governments face the need to raise revenues in order to invest in education, infrastructure, or other enhancements to the economy's long-term productivity. Selling public assets is one way of bridging the revenue gap.

The growing international indebtedness of many developing countries, which was reaching crisis proportions by the early 1980s, forced them to seek ways of raising capital and of trimming current expenditures by selling off loss-making public enterprises. One of the countries that has placed the most direct emphasis on debt reduction is Argentina. It has even permitted purchasers of SOEs to buy up Argentine external and internal debt obligations on the secondary market at a discount and to apply them to the purchase price of the SOE in "debt-equity swaps."

In instituting its program of debt-equity swaps, Argentina was responding partly to pressure from the international banking community, particularly the World Bank and the International Monetary Fund (IMF). These agencies made new loans to Argentina on the condition that Argentina implement a privatization program whose receipts would be used to reduce the country's US$60 billion international debt. The Brady Plan for restructuring Argentina's external debt also required that the government obtain a certain level of receipts from privatization and pay US$400 million in back interest to the banks. The receipts from the sale of the state telephone and electricity monopolies enabled it to meet the first condition, and the cash for the interest arrears came directly from the proceeds of the Gas del Estado divestiture.[1]

OBJECTIVES OF LOCAL GOVERNMENT OFFICIALS

Government officials at the regional or local level have interests in privatization that are analogous, but not necessarily parallel, to those of the national government. Indeed, to some extent, their interests may be opposed to those of the national government. For example, the national privatization program may be intended to reduce the national debt, to trim operating subsidies to SOEs, and to increase overall economic efficiency. However, many of the economic benefits of privatization to the national economy may be lost on local governments (unless the latter are the owners of the enterprises themselves), who are fearful of the

---

[1] John Williams and Richard Morse, "Argentina: Going from Strength to Strength," *Privatization Yearbook* 1993 (London: Privatisation International Ltd., 1993), p. 170.

potential local unemployment consequences of privatization.

Under such circumstances, the logical political strategy for local elected officials might be to come out in opposition to privatization, in order to win the favor of an anxious electorate. In addition to their concern for the local economy and the interests of their constituents, the opposition of some local government officials to privatization may have deeper, ideological roots. Particularly in the former Socialist countries, the process of purging governments of former Communists may not have completely reached the local government level. Even if they are forced to disguise their political beliefs to suit the changing times, some prominent local officials remain committed in principle to the old system of state control of the economy.

OBJECTIVES OF SOE MANAGERS

The top management of most SOEs sees privatization as an opportunity, or at least they see the handwriting on the wall and are determined to make the most of it. Many managers do not wait for government action before they begin to court potential investors, particularly foreign firms. The more progressive managers view private (especially foreign) investors as a source of needed capital, technology, know-how, and access to markets, without which their companies are doomed to wither and probably die.

SOE management's unique perspective holds the potential for conflict with the government privatization authorities. For example, management may be interested in an alliance with a foreign company in order to gain access to that company's technology and marketing channels. The government, on the other hand, may favor the distribution of a larger percentage of the shares to the population at large through a voucher scheme, employees, and various social funds than SOE management or its prospective partner would favor.

Whether or not they are progressive, most managers naturally have a tendency to evaluate different privatization alternatives from the perspective of the effect that it will have on their own career prospects. Some are prepared to buy a controlling interest in the company themselves, if they can secure financing. Others merely wish to ensure that the new private owners have a place for them in their personnel plans.

Management's interest in securing its own position need not pose a problem if it is committed and capable of running the enterprise. The challenge for the potential investor in such cases is to find ways of working with SOE management, without sacrificing overall control of the company. However, if SOE management sees its future as threatened by the privatization project, they may try to sabotage or preempt the process.

OBJECTIVES OF SOE EMPLOYEES

Workers may be fearful of losing their jobs or some of their job-related benefits as part of a privatization-related enterprise restructuring. In countries whose laws give workers a significant voice in the running of their SOEs, worker opposition can make privatization more difficult.

Many workers are interested in purchasing shares in their company, provided a way of financing the purchase can be found. Employee stock purchase plans have helped to win employees and their unions over to privatization, and are usually in the long-term interest of the company, in that they give employees a stake in the company's future.

BUILDING A CONSTITUENCY FOR PRIVATIZATION

It follows from this discussion that the investor needs to understand who the key actors in the privatization process are and the relative importance each of them attaches to the various objectives. A large part of the spadework for a prospective investment in an SOE involves talking to all of the different stakeholders and ensuring that the investment project will respond as fully as possible to their interests, in a manner that is consistent with the investor's overall strategy. An investment project that does not take into account the different interest groups' positions stands a high likelihood of failure.

CHAPTER 3

Methods of Privatization

Governments use a variety of mechanisms for transferring public assets and services to private investors. The main mechanisms include the following:

- *Auction:* The SOE's assets are sold to the highest bidder in open bidding.

- *Negotiated sale:* The price and terms of the transaction are agreed to in direct negotiations between the buyer and the seller.

- *Tender:* Bidders submit sealed bids, which are opened at an announced time, with the property generally going to the highest bidder.

- *Stock flotation:* The government's shares are offered on local or international capital markets.

- *Management/employee buyout:* SOE management and/or employees buy a controlling interest in the company.

- *Stock distribution:* A percentage of shares (generally in the 10–25 percent range) in the SOE are given or sold at preferential terms to employees and other special groups such as former political prisoners.

- *Voucher or coupon privatization:* Eligible citizens are given or are sold coupons or vouchers at a nominal price, which can be exchanged for shares in former state-owned companies or in investment funds that control the actual company shares.

In addition to an outright transfer of ownership, there are other mechanisms by which many of the same objectives as outright privatization can be achieved such as the following:

- *Joint venture:* The private investor and the SOE join forces to form a distinct legal entity, but one that preserves the distinction between public and private capital.

- *Build-own-operate-and-transfer (BOOT) agreements:* Such agreements are used mainly for infrastructure projects. The private investor pays the cost of constructing a toll road, bridge, or facility and then is entitled to collect a share of the revenues for an agreed-upon period of time (say, 20 years), after which time ownership reverts to the government.

- *Leasing:* The private investor pays the government an agreed-upon annual fee to operate an SOE or other publicly owned facility but is entitled to keep the balance of the operating profits.

- *Management contract:* The government pays a private operator an agreed-upon fee to operate an SOE or other facility.

The range of privatization mechanisms available to a government is usually defined by law. However, governments nearly always have several mechanisms available to them and will choose the mechanism to privatize a particular SOE according to its specific characteristics, as well as exogenous factors, such as political considerations.

AUCTION

Auctions so far have been used mostly for small businesses, such as retail shops and service establishments, which, in general, are of little interest to foreign investors. In Eastern Europe and the former Soviet republics, tens, if not hundreds, of thousands of such auctions have been conducted. In many cases, the state employees who ran these shops or establishments are given the first chance to bid for them, before the bidding is opened to other investors.

There have been some cases of a state-owned medium or large enterprise (MLE) being liquidated and its assets sold at auction, particularly in the developing countries. There are plenty of MLEs around that are not commercially viable entities but that possess auctionable assets, such as prime real estate or up-to-date equipment. However, relatively few of these enterprises have come up on the auction block so far.

In the short to medium term, the emphasis in most MLE privatization programs has been on divesting those SOEs that are potentially viable under free market conditions, with or without restructuring, and that can be sold as a going concern. In the early stages of a country's privatization program, it is vital for the government to establish a track record of successful privatizations in order to generate political support for the program and to stimulate investor interest. These SOEs have the best chance of finding suitable buyers quickly and of succeeding as private enterprises.

Moreover, since these SOEs are privatized as going concerns, the new owners are likely to retain at least a percentage of the work force, mitigating the unemployment and
other adverse economic impacts of a shutdown.

Similarly, governments are likely to put off as long as possible the difficult decision to close the gates of most non-
viable enterprises. However, in the longer term, we may see
more cases of medium and large SOEs' assets being sold at
auction.

NEGOTIATED SALES

In a negotiated sale, the SOE and/or its owners (i.e., the
government) negotiate directly with a single investor for the
transfer of all or a share of the SOE's equity to the investor.
In some cases, the parties are brought to the negotiating
table by an investment bank or other financial intermediary.
In other cases, the negotiations are the result of direct contacts between the prospective seller and buyer. Some countries, such as the Czech Republic, even allow investors to
propose their own programs for privatizing an SOE.

A few countries, such as Germany, have made extensive
use of negotiated sales to divest their SOEs. However, as a
rule, negotiated sales are less common than other types of
transactions and, when they are used, tend to be reserved
for large "flagship" SOEs.

From the seller's point of view, there are several disad-
vantages associated with a negotiated sale. First, a negotiated sale is widely regarded as too time-consuming,
although, as we shall see in Chapter 5, this is not necessarily
the case. Second, it tends to result in a lower selling price
than a tender, because the element of competition is absent.
Third, because the negotiations take place out of the public
view, there is the possibility that opponents of the government or of the privatization process will try to make political

capital by accusing the government's negotiators of settling for a lower price than they could have gotten, or even of financial improprieties.

TENDER

Unlike an auction, which as a rule is used to dispose of the assets of an SOE in liquidation, a tender often is used to divest SOEs that are going concerns. In a tender privatization, prospective investors in an SOE submit their bids in sealed envelopes, which are opened publicly at an announced time and place.

Many governments prefer tenders because of their relative simplicity and ease of implementation. Tenders also, in general, result in higher prices than negotiated sales, due to the element of competition. Governments using tenders also feel less vulnerable to politically motivated accusations of poor negotiating performance or improprieties in negotiations, because the tender process is conducted in the public eye according to predetermined guidelines.

STOCK FLOTATION

Public share offerings have been used widely, especially in the developed market economies, to dispose of the government's interest in SOEs. The British government, for example, used this technique to sell millions of shares in British Telecom, British Gas, and the ten water companies.

While public share offerings are most common in the developed countries, they are by no means limited to these countries. For example, Nigeria has privatized thirty-five SOEs via public share offerings, and Sri Lanka has conducted several very successful share offerings since 1989. Chile, Jamaica, and the Philippines are other examples of countries that have used public share offerings to divest SOEs. However, the capital markets in most of the post-Socialist and developing countries are either nonexistent or too shallow to support extensive use of this type of privatization. Most of their SOEs are also in too poor a condition to be fit for stock flotation.[1]

MANAGEMENT/EMPLOYEE BUYOUT (M/EBO)

By definition, an M/EBO is not directly relevant to foreign investors, unless management and employees are competing with the prospective investor to buy a controlling share of the SOE. M/EBOs have been used sporadically in a number of countries. In Russia, however, they are quite common.[2] In addition to the standard distribution of shares (25 percent of capital transferred free of charge to workers as preferred shares, with the right to buy an additional 10 percent as ordinary shares at a 30 percent discount, and up to 5 percent of shares sold to management as ordinary shares at par), Russian law provides that managers and workers between them can buy ordinary (voting) shares, representing up to 51 percent of the capital of an SOE by closed subscription. The price is equal to the book value of the shares multiplied by 1.7, that is, a nominal price. Up to 50 percent of the shares can be purchased with vouchers.

STOCK DISTRIBUTION

A number of countries' privatization laws mandate that a certain percentage (typically 10 percent but sometimes as

---

[1] Sunita Kikeri, John Nellis, and Mary Shirley, *Privatization: The Lessons of Experience* (Washington, DC: The World Bank, 1992), p. 55.
[2] Elena Kotova, Andrey Vasiliev, and Alexander Abramov, "Management and Employee Buy-Outs in Russia."

much as 25 percent) of the shares of each SOE being privatized should be given to their workers or sold to them at a discount. Financing is often provided to those workers who are unable to afford shares. On balance, such programs are beneficial to private investors, because they help blunt employee opposition to privatization and give employees a stake in the efficient running of the privatized enterprise.

VOUCHER OR COUPON PRIVATIZATION

Poland pioneered the concept of mass privatization, although it has taken Poland longer than other countries, such as the Czech Republic, to get its mass privatization program going. In the Czech Republic's mass privatization program, all adult citizens were given the opportunity to purchase vouchers at the deeply discounted price of about US$35, which could be exchanged for shares in privatized SOEs that had elected to participate in the mass privatization program, either directly or through an "investment fund." To some extent, there may be an implicit contradiction between the aims of mass privatization, which is to spread ownership of former SOEs as widely as possible, and the private investor's interest in securing sufficient control over the SOE to implement a restructuring program.

In practice, different nations' mass privatization programs have dealt with this implicit contradiction in various ways. For instance, in the Czech Republic, SOEs and other interested parties were invited to submit privatization proposals to the government, in which they were to propose the percentage of shares to be sold through various avenues, including the voucher program. In the first "wave" of 1,200 MLEs to be privatized, approximately 50 percent of the total shares were sold via the voucher program, indicating that many companies were holding shares back in the hope of finding a "strategic" investor.[3]

Russia is virtually alone in requiring foreign investors in privatized SOEs to purchase vouchers at auction, just like ordinary Russians. This requirement is probably the main reason why there have been almost no foreign equity investments in Russian SOEs. Instead, investors have gone the route of forming joint ventures with their SOE counterparts, freeing them from the potential risk and management headaches associated with voucher privatization.

JOINT VENTURE

In a joint venture, the private investor and the SOE each contribute assets to a new entity, as defined in the joint venture agreement. For the private investor, it is a way of reducing financial outlays and, consequently, risk.

For example, U.S. Windpower (a manufacturer of wind turbines for generating electricity) formed a joint venture with Ukraine's state-owned electric utility Krimenergo in order to develop wind power applications in the Crimean Peninsula. If the venture meets its founders' expectations, it should allow Krimenergo to shut down the Chernobyl nuclear power station, site of a catastrophic accident in 1986.

U.S. Windpower will design and engineer the wind turbines. Krimenergo will pay for the technology in windmill parts that will be manufactured at a former Soviet tank plant. U.S. Windpower officials declined to place a value on the joint venture because of the nonconvertibility of the Ukrainian currency, but a comparable

---

[3] *Privatization Newsletter of Czechoslovakia*, August–September 1992, Table 4, p. 5.

venture in the United States would be worth US$500 million.[4]

BUILD-OWN-OPERATE-AND-TRANSFER (BOOT) AGREEMENTS

BOOTs are used mainly for large energy and infrastructure projects. The investors find the financing and build and operate the facility for a fixed period of time. They recover their initial capital outlay plus a reasonable return by charging user fees. At the end of the contract, ownership reverts to the government.

The government of Malaysia awarded a concession to a private company, United Engineers Malaysia, to build and operate the 900-kilometer North-South Expressway. The total cost of the project was US$3.5 billion. In return, the concessionaire receives the right to collect and retain all vehicle tolls for thirty years. In addition, the government agreed to reduce the concessionaire's risks by making up any shortfall in the projected traffic volume for the first seventeen years, as well as offsetting any adverse changes in the foreign exchange rate or external loan interest charges.[5]

LEASING

Leases and concessions are similar, in that the lessee or concessionaire pays either a fixed fee or a percentage of profits for the right to operate a facility or to provide a service, keeping the rest of the proceeds. Leases typically refer to

---

[4] *Eastern Europe Reporter*, Vol. 3, No. 3 (March 1, 1993), p. 179.

[5] Matthew L. Hensley and Edward P. White, "The Privatization Experience in Malaysia," *Columbia Journal of World Business*, Vol. 28, No. 1 (Spring 1993), p. 81.

natural resources or manufacturing plants, while concessions refer to a public service or other activity.

After failing to find a private buyer for a loss-making
steel mini-mill, the government of Togo agreed to lease it to
a privately owned company for a fixed annual fee during
the first two years and an increasing share of the gross mar-
gin (up to 40 percent in year 6 and thereafter) for the
remainder of the lease. The Togolese authorities, for their
part, agreed to exempt the company from all import and
export duties, to freeze import duties and taxes on competing imported products at existing levels for five years, and
to make foreign exchange available for equipment and
input purchases, and the repatriation of profits and dividends.[6]

The city of Buenos Aires has been granting concessions
with a vengeance. Concessionaires issue parking tickets and
collect fines, enforce vehicle safety standards, collect taxes,
and run markets, sports arenas, and even the municipal zoo
for a profit.[7]

MANAGEMENT CONTRACT

In a management contract, a private firm receives a fixed
fee from the governmental entity to operate a public facility
or to provide a service. The water systems of Abidjan and
other cities in the Ivory Coast are operated and maintained
under contract by a company with French and Ivoirien
shareholders.

---

[6] Ivan Bergeron, "Privatization Through Leasing: The Togo Steel
Case," in Ravi Ramamurti and Raymond Vernon (eds.), *Privatization and
Control of State-Owned Enterprises* (Washington, DC: The World Bank,
1991), pp. 153–175.

[7] *Privatisation International* (November 1990), p. 22.

COMBINED MECHANISMS

For many SOEs, several of these mechanisms are used in combination. We mentioned the case of the Czech Republic, where SOEs and prospective investors are invited to submit privatization proposals that draw on a whole menu of privatization mechanisms: direct sale, management buyout, stock flotation, voucher privatization, and so forth. Other governments, for instance Sri Lanka, have adopted what amounts to a formula for dividing shareholdings in most SOEs: so many shares to the employees, so many shares to the general public via the stock market, and so many shares to the "core" investor, who will take on the actual restructuring and running of the firm.

CHAPTER 4

Worldwide Experience in Privatization

In the general excitement over the political and economic transformation of the former Soviet Union and Central and Eastern Europe, one tends to lose sight of the progress that privatization has made in other parts of the world. Figure 4-1 gives a general idea of the geographical distribution of privatizations during the 1980s and and early 1990s. The figures on which Exhibit 4-1 are based include only medium and large enterprises (MLEs), which are the type of SOE of greatest interest to potential foreign investors.

EASTERN EUROPE AND THE FORMER SOVIET UNION

We should begin our discussion of Figure 4-1 by noting that the statistics for Eastern Europe, on which it is based, omit the former East Germany, because the capital and human resources that the German government has been able to devote to restructuring and privatization make its situation

FIGURE 4-1 Number of privatizations by region, 1980–1991

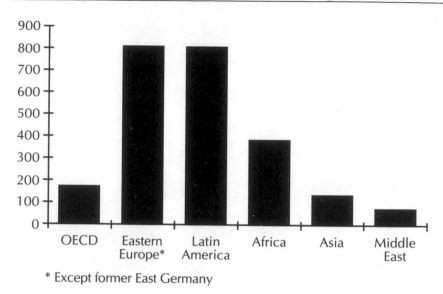

* Except former East Germany

Source: S. Kikeri, J. Nellis and M. Shirley, *Privatization: The Lessons of Experience* (Washington, DC: The World Bank, 1992), p. 22.

unique. As a result, Germany was able to privatize some 4,500 former SOEs in its eastern zone by 1991. By 1993, Germany's privatization agency, the Treuhand, was on the verge of wrapping up its work of disposing 8,000 former East German SOEs and was hoping to assist other governments' privatization programs on a consulting basis. Figure 4-1 also does not reflect significant developments since 1992, such as the start of the Czech voucher privatization program and the acceleration of the Russian privatization program.

If Germany is omitted, Hungary and the Czech Republic are the MLE privatization leaders in Central and Eastern Europe. Until 1992, Hungary had the best privatization track record in Central and Eastern Europe after Germany, with as many as 500–600 privatizations completed through March 1992. However, the Czech Republic has become a serious contender with its mass privatization of 1,200 SOEs in 1992, followed by another 1,200 privatizations in 1993. Mass privatization has enabled the Czechs to speed up the privatization process by making SOEs responsible for preparing their own privatizing plans and by selling tradable, low-cost vouchers to citizens who would then exchange them for shares in privatized companies as described on page 23.

Although Poland has privatized over 80 percent of its small retail and trade outlets, it managed to privatize only twenty-six MLEs by the end of 1991. In 1992, the Polish government planned to "accelerate" the pace of privatization to 40–50 MLEs. Poland was the cradle of the mass privatization concept, but political controversy prevented a mass privatization scheme from being enacted into law until mid-1993.

The pace of privatization has been slower in the rest of the region. The continuing civil war in what used to be Yugoslavia has put a damper on privatization efforts, with the limited exception of Slovenia, which has hardly been involved in the fighting. The distressed state of the Romanian and Bulgarian economies, combined with political instability, has prevented privatization from really getting off the ground. Albania, the former "Tibet of Europe" is pretty much sui generis, but it, too, has set up a privatization agency and is poised to pass a law on privatization.

Privatization in what was formerly the Soviet Union had scarcely gotten off the ground when the figures shown in Figure 4-1 were compiled. By 1993, however, not only had most shops, restaurants and small businesses passed into private hands, but also—at least in the Russian republic—MLE privatization was picking up steam. By the end of March 1993, more than 1,000 MLEs had either completed or announced auctions in the country's mass privatization program. Most foreign investors have elected to form joint ventures or start new enterprises, reflecting the administrative difficulties and perceived risks of investing in Russian SOEs.

LATIN AMERICA

As Figure 4-1 shows, Latin America (including the Caribbean) rivaled Central and Eastern Europe (minus Germany) in the number of enterprises privatized through 1991, with 804 privatizations versus 805 for Central and Eastern Europe. Development of active capital markets in a number of countries and a renewed interest in attracting foreign capital and investment have stimulated the privatization process region-wide.

Chile and Mexico have been the leaders in privatization in Latin America. Chile's privatization program, which essentially fell into two phases, began during the mid-1970s. From 1974 to 1978, the country's military-led government privatized 207 companies, which yielded $ 1.2 billion in revenues for the government. The government relied on three privatization methods during this phase, that is, liquidation, direct sales, and auction.

Buyers of SOEs at Chile's auctions during the 1970s were not checked for solvency, experience, or general management capabilities. Because of a general lack of liquidity in the economy, following a highly inflationary period, sales were made on credit. As privatized businesses faltered, the government failed to collect on payments, and banks, which had extended credit liberally, faltered. The lessons from this experience led to a second, more successful phase of privatizations during the mid-1980s, and, by the end of the decade, the Chilean government maintained control of fewer than 50 of the approximately 600 enterprises it had owned during the 1970s.

Faced with a growing economic crisis in 1982, Mexico undertook a far-reaching program of macroeconomic reform coupled with privatization of small- to medium-sized enterprises. As reforms took hold, divestiture of larger SOEs was initiated. By the end of 1992, the government of Mexico had sold off 961 out of the 1,155 enterprises that it had owned in 1982. (This figure is not directly comparable with the number of privatizations shown in Figure 4-1 because it includes small privatizations.)

Argentina's privatization program also has been gaining momentum. According to one source, Argentina had succeeded in privatizing only 5 percent of its SOEs, worth US$1.5 billion, by 1991,[1] but, in 1992 alone, the government sold its stake in Telecom Argentina for US$1.2 billion; SEGBA, the electric utility, for US$1.05 billion; and Gas del Estado for over US$3 billion. Other sales in 1992 included various oil, highway, and railway concessions; television channels; petrochemical plants; steelworks; shipyards; and Obras Sanitarias de la Nacion, Argentina's national water pipeline system. Privatizations planned for 1993 include Caja Nacionale de Ahorro y Seguro, the state savings bank and insurance company; Transenerg, the national electricity transmission system; the state oil company; the postal service; and the national mint.[2]

Venezuela also has been pursuing privatization as a part of its structural adjustment program. The Venezuelan government initiated privatization activities in 1989 and has already generated over US$2.34 billion in revenues through the privatization of twenty-two SOEs.Venezuela has relied on a variety of mechanisms to implement its privatizations, including transfer of property through sale of assets or sale of shares, transfer of administration through concessions, and privatization of construction and/or operation of infra-

---

[1] Sunita Kikeri, John Nellis, and Mary Shirley, *Privatization: The Lessons of Experience* (Washington, D.C.: The World Bank, 1992), pp. 25, 30.

[2] John Williams and Richard Morse, "Argentina: Going from Strength to Strength," *Privatisation Yearbook 1993*, p. 171.

structure. Among the enterprises to be privatized in 1993 are the largest electric generation plant in Latin America, the Caracas racetrack, and a number of resort hotels.

While some countries have been more aggressive than others in pursuing privatization programs, the increasingly successful implementation of these programs has served to stimulate the interest of those countries that have been slower to act, such as Peru, Ecuador, and Brazil. Most Latin American countries now have active privatization programs, with a few exceptions, such as Paraguay and Uruguay, where privatization was stopped after Uruguayan voters rejected it in a December 1992 referendum.

SUB-SAHARAN AFRICA

Sub-Saharan Africa is one of the areas that has the most to gain from privatization. The idea that the public sector is the appropriate catalyst for economic development took root deeply in Africa. After the end of colonial rule, African governments moved to take control of their economies and to protect industry from the perceived outside interference of Western multinationals. Large industrial concerns were nationalized, and, during the 1960s and 1970s, state-owned enterprises became the rule, rather than the exception.

Now, however, as leaders of African governments move to tackle budget deficits and to stimulate economic activity, they are looking to privatization as a tool for stimulating economic growth. They are supported by development banks, such as the World Bank and the African Development Bank, which have made privatization a vital component of their economic reform packages in Africa.

According to the World Bank, there were nearly 3,000 SOEs in thirty countries of Sub-Saharan Africa by the mid-

1980s.[3] Of these, 337 were privatized through 1991, which represented 17 percent of the worldwide total. Guinea was reportedly the leader, with over 60 privatizations, which is not so surprising in view of the fact that Guinea had more SOEs in 1980—180 of them—than any country in Africa except Senegal and Tanzania. Nigeria, which has the largest economy in Africa, came in second, with about 50 privatizations through 1991. In addition, in a move to increase self-sufficiency, the Nigerian government cut subsidies to public enterprises by 50 percent across the board.

The Ivory Coast has also been actively privatizing its SOEs and has used a somewhat unconventional means of targeting potential enterprises for privatization. Rather than designate candidates for sale, the government has indicated that it is willing to consider offers for any enterprise deemed an attractive investment by private companies. Using this method, the government has divested itself of nearly 30 enterprises, most of which are industrial or agro-industrial concerns. Means of privatization have included management buy-outs (MBOs), initial public offerings (IPOs), and foreign investments.

THE MIDDLE EAST

The Middle East, including Africa north of the Sahara, accounted for only fifty-eight privatizations during the period 1980–1991, or 1 percent of the total (see Figure 4-1), despite the fact that some Middle Eastern countries, such as Egypt and Iran, have relatively large public sectors. The Iranian government's plans to privatize many SOEs have been delayed because of the opposition of influential clerics who head the various state holding companies.

---

[3] John R. Nellis, *Public Enterprises in Sub-Saharan Africa* (Washington, DC: The World Bank, 1986), p. 5.

In Saudi Arabia, the slow pace of privatization is also due to opposition from religious groups, as well as private business interests' penchant for secrecy, which makes them suspicious of the filings and disclosures that are usually involved in the purchase of an SOE.[4] Due to bureaucratic foot-dragging, Egypt did not put its first lot of sixteen SOEs—eight of them hotels—up for sale until the spring of 1993.[5] Algeria announced a sweeping privatization program amid great fanfare in 1992, but initial skepticism of most observers has deepened with the continuing political unrest in that country.[6]

ASIA

Through 1991, Asia had a relatively small number of privatizations (122, or 2 percent of the total). Those Asian countries with the largest public sectors, that is, China, India, Vietnam, and North Korea, have not begun large-scale privatization programs. However, there are indications that these countries may begin to initiate privatization programs in the near future. For example, Vietnam recently hired an adviser to work on designing a program for the privatization of its 700 SOEs.[7]

China has begun to develop a securities market, and a number of Chinese SOEs have begun to raise capital by selling shares to domestic and foreign investors. In 1992, twenty-two companies were listed in Shanghai and sixteen

---

[4] Pamela Ann Smith, "Gulf States Reorientate Towards Private Sector," *Privatisation International*, No. 42 (March 1992), p. 1.

[5] "Good Response to Egypt's First Offers," *Privatisation International*, No. 56 (May 1993), p. 1.

[6] Pamela Ann Smith, "Algeria Widens Plan," *Privatisation International*, No. 45 (June 1992), p. 2.

[7] Vietnam May Sell 700 Firms," *Privatisation International*, No. 40 (January 1992), p. 10.

were listed in Shenzhen. At present, the government retains a majority interest in most of these companies, and senior members of the Communist party generally sit on each company's board of directors.[8] As well-known and respected Western financial institutions (e.g., Swiss Bank and Merrill Lynch) begin to take part in China's securities market, it is generally accepted that the trend toward promotion of at least partial privatization of SOEs will continue in China. China's move to institute privatization may set an example for other Asian countries with large public sectors.

Elsewhere in Asia, the newly industrialized countries (NICs)—South Korea, Taiwan, Hong Kong, and Singapore—have seen little privatization activity for the simple reason that they do not have many SOEs. Other countries in the region, such as Malaysia, the Philippines, and Sri Lanka, have ongoing privatization programs. Sri Lanka has achieved an impressive record of privatizations (twenty-four as of the end of 1992), while building popular support for the privatization program by gifting 10 percent of the shares of each SOE to employees at divestiture and selling significant tranches of stock (about 30 percent of each SOE, on average) in the local stock market.[9]

As the other economies of Asia, such as those of Malaysia, Thailand, and the Philippines, attempt to emulate the growth and development of the NICs, privatization is likely to continue apace. The NICs have proven that market-driven growth can be wildly successful. In addition, if, in fact, privatization takes off in China, it is likely that the other traditionally Socialist economies in the region will fol-

---

[8] "China Looks Outward," *Privatisation International*, No. 45 (June 1992), p. 1.

[9] Tissa Jayasinghe, "Sri Lanka: Combination of Economic and Social Goals," *Privatization Yearbook 1993*, (London: Privatisation International, 1993), pp. 262–265.

low suit. Thus, it will not be surprising if the pace of Asian privatization accelerates through the rest of the 1990s.

OECD COUNTRIES

Privatization has also lagged in many developed countries of the OECD (Organization for Economic Cooperation and Development). Of the OECD countries, which include the nations of Western Europe, North America, and Japan, SOEs on the whole represent a relatively low portion of (GDP). Thus, there are proportionately fewer candidates for privatization within the nations of the OECD.

Among the OECD countries, none has gone as far as Great Britain in privatizing state-owned assets. Since 1979, Great Britain has sold more than one-half of its state-owned industrial assets, valued at over US$70 billion. Other European states, notably France and Italy, have held back. This situation may change, as European Community (EC) policies requiring governments to provide a "level playing field" for private enterprise make state ownership less attractive.[10]

The EC policies coincide with a shift in the political center of gravity in a number of European "social democracies," which may lead to an acceleration in the pace of privatization. As is the case in developing and middle-income countries around the world, the governments of these countries are looking to privatization as a means of shedding unwanted financial and managerial obligations, and of increasing government revenues during a period of government deficits.

The advent of a center-right government in France was accompanied by a bill establishing the framework for the new government's privatization program. In May 1993, the

---

[10] "EC Policies Point Towards the Private Sector," *Privatisation International*, No. 43 (April 1992), p.1.

newly elected French government announced a far-reaching privatization program. Although France has tried to undertake privatization before, this is the most comprehensive program announced to date. Touching on twenty-one financial, industrial, and manufacturing companies, it expects to raise approximately US$7.25 billion in revenues in 1993 alone. More revenues will follow—tens of billions of dollars, according to the government—as the program is implemented over a period of years.

Likewise, the German government has announced its intention to privatize a number of state-run operations outside the country's eastern zone, either wholly or partially, in the coming years. Facing skyrocketing bills in the wake of unification, the traditionally economically conservative German government is scrambling to cover its costs by corporatizing and selling off shares in such organizations as the Deutschebundespost and Deutschebundesbahn—the German postal and rail systems, respectively.

Other European nations are following this trend, sharing in the hope that streamlining the government outflow and payroll will prove to be a means of fiscal stabilization. Even traditionally Socialist Sweden has been pursuing privatization more energetically since the right-of-center Bildt government took power from the Social Democrats.

Outside Europe, OECD countries, including the United States and Japan, are likely to continue selective privatization of state-run entities. In the United States, state and local governments, faced with near-crippling deficits and funding requirements, are introducing innovative means of encouraging the private management of activities that traditionally have been part of the government's domain. These include moves to contract out provision of public services, as well as introduction of build-own-operate-and-transfer (BOOT) infrastructure projects.

As the Japanese government faces an increasingly sluggish economy, it, too, may turn to private management and ownership of enterprises. Meanwhile, the European members of the OECD which are already undertaking privatization programs will likely press forward with these, through the end of the decade.

In general, while many of the observations about privatization in this book are as true of the OECD countries as they are of the post-Socialist and developing countries, it is the latter group of countries that form the primary focus of this book (see Box 4-1).

BOX 4-1　Privatization in the Developed Market Economies

This book focuses on privatization opportunities outside the OECD countries. The main reason for this focus is that most of the opportunities for this book's intended audiences (i.e., the potential equity investor with little prior experience in privatization), are located in the post-Socialist and developing countries, rather than the IMEs (Industrial Market Economies). As noted in Chapter 4, the privatization programs of a number of important IMEs, such as France and Italy, have barely gotten off the ground. In most other developed countries, the majority of privatizations have been very large transactions, conducted via direct sales or public share offerings. In the case of direct sales, major corporate investors have been the target, whereas in the case of public share offerings, portfolio investors, including small individual investors, have been the target.

In addition, much of what we have said about privatization in the post-Socialist and developing nations is generally applicable to privatization in the IMEs as well. This is not to say there are no differences at all. In addition to a greater reliance on financial market mechanisms to transfer ownership of state assets to the private sector, other differences between privatization in IMEs versus other nations includes the following;

- *More investment alternatives:* The prospective investor has more alternatives to investing in an SOE in the diversified economy of most IMEs, such as buying an interest in a private concern.

- *Higher prices:* Prices of SOEs in IMEs tend to be higher in relation to their market value than SOE prices elsewhere, meaning that there are much fewer "bargains" to be had.
- *Less risk:* In the final choice of investment target, the country's risks (particularly political risks) of investing in an IME SOE are less material ones than characteristics of the individual company or companies.
- *Companies more of a "known quantity":* The company risks associated with SOEs in the developed market economies are more readily quantifiable than other SOEs, because they have a track record of competing in a market-based economy.
- *Market-based valuation mechanisms:* Market-based mechanisms exist for assigning a value to SOE assets in developed countries.
- *Less restructuring reguired:* The typical developed-country SOE requires less post-privatization restructuring to put it on a competitive footing than its post-Socialist or developing-country counterpart.

The United States is a special case, in that it does not have any SOEs in the classic sense. Virtually all of the privatization that is taking place in the United States is in the areas of infrastructure and public services.

The Federal Office of Privatization has been reported at times as having several privatization initiatives underway, including a sale of power stations by the Alaska Power Marketing Administration and leasing of the Naval Petroleum Reserves. In the future, other projects might include the privatization of power marketing rights for the Southeast Power Administration, the National Weather Service, Amtrak, the Rural Electrification Agency, unassigned radio spectrum controlled by the federal government, uranium enrichment, and federal prison leasing."[11]

However, most privatization initiatives in the United States have been at the state and local levels. The potential scope for such privatizations was expanded by Executive Order 12803 of April 30, 1992, on infrastructure privatization. This order enables state and local governments to sell or lease public facilities built with federal financial assistance without having to return most of the revenues to the

---

[11] *Privatisation International*, August 1990, p. 16.

federal government, and it directs the relevant federal agencies to cooperate fully with state and local requests to privatize.

In response, a number of state and local governments are studying infrastructure privatization proposals. In particular, a lot of attention has been given to privatizing municipal wastewater treatment plants. The U.S. Environmental Protection Agency (EPA) has been encouraging this interest through seminars and a pilot program. Indianapolis recently became the first city to submit an application to the EPA to sell or lease its wastewater facilities. There are a number of U.S. firms that specialize in operating wastewater plants under short-term contracts.

Airport privatization is also in vogue in the United States. Projects under discussion include the sale or lease of Los Angeles International Airport.

Another important piece of federal enabling legislation has been the Intermodal Surface Transportation Efficiency Act (ISTEA), which allows states to levy tolls on existing and new federally aided bridges, roads, and tunnels. ISTEA should facilitate privately financed infrastructure schemes such as BOOT (build-own-operate-and-transfer) projects. Various states are pushing through legislation to enable them to take advantage of ISTEA's provisions. One of the projects that is most advanced is the proposed Dulles Toll Road Extension outside Washington, D.C.

In spite of these developments, it is still the contracting out of various public services that accounts for the bulk of privatization activity in the United States. Contracting out has been applied successfully for some time to such services as municipal transit and trash collection. Among the more innovative applications that have surfaced recently are child-support collection, educational services, and correctional facilities.

Privatization of state and local services has been opposed by the American Federation of State, County, and Municipal Employees (AFSCME). However, it is considered unlikely that President Clinton will respond to the union's calls to rescind the Executive Order 12803 on infrastructure privatization. Indeed, the administration's campaign to "reinvent government" may lead to further, imaginative proposals for the privatization of activities and services formerly performed by the government.[12]

---

[12] *Privatisation Yearbook 1993* and *Privatisation International* (various issues).

CHAPTER 5

The Making of a Successful Privatization Program

Why are some countries' privatization programs so much more effective in divesting SOEs than others'? This question is important to governments as well as to potential investors, who have an interest in seeing their proposed investment in an SOE consummated as quickly and easily as possible. The answer depends, in part, on the type of SOE we are talking about. In the case of small SOEs (e.g., shops, service establishments), tens of thousands of them have been privatized through auctions in Eastern Europe and the former Soviet republics. However, these are not the type of SOEs that interest most foreign investors, who naturally tend to focus on medium or large enterprises. MLEs also represent the bulk of state-owned assets in most countries.

As the point of departure for our discussion, let us compare the experiences of five countries that have enjoyed

FIGURE 5-1   Examples of successful privatization programs
(percentage of medium and large SOEs
privatized through 1993)

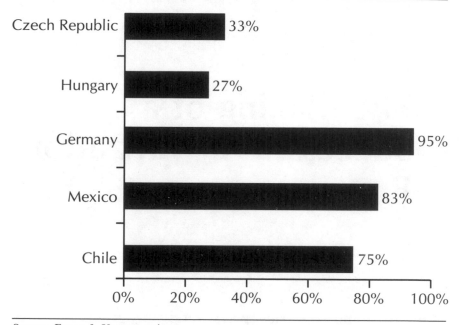

Source: Ernst & Young estimates.

considerable success in privatizing their medium or large SOEs: Germany, the Czech Republic, Hungary, Chile, and Mexico (see Figure 5-1).

What traits do these countries have in common that may have contributed to their success? Possible answers include:

- A comparatively strong economy

- A viable private sector

- A common approach to privatization

- Favorable legal and institutional factors

In the rest of this chapter, we will examine each of these factors in turn.

ECONOMIC CONDITIONS

Current economic conditions in all of these countries are obviously relatively favorable compared with the majority of privatizing countries, other than the OECD countries. Despite the pressures of unification, Germany is in a uniquely favorable position as one of the world's richest nations, with a large home market of German investors. The other four nations in Figure 5-1 all rank near the top of the so-called middle-income countries.

However, we should not place exclusive emphasis on the role of countries' relatively strong economies in propelling their privatization programs forward. Hungary, the Czech Republic, Chile, and Mexico all inaugurated their programs at a time when they were in the midst of making major structural adjustments in their economic programs.

Hungary and the Czech Republic (then Czechoslovakia) were trying to reorient their economies away from the old Soviet trading bloc toward full membership in the world market economy. Czechoslovakia itself was in the process of breaking up into two countries, posing the threat of further economic disruption. Chile was in the throes of a severe economic, social, and political crisis following the military's overthrow of the avowedly Marxist regime of President Salvador Allende. Mexico was grappling with an international debt crisis and skyrocketing inflation.

What is perhaps more important than a burgeoning local economy is a sense of optimism about the future; that is, the government is taking the steps needed to place the national economy on a path of long-term growth.

A VIABLE PRIVATE SECTOR

The stronger the country's private sector is, in general, the better are the prospects for privatization. The existence of a viable private sector in itself is an indication that the "enabling environment" meets the minimum needs for successful privatization.

The privatization program in Germany has benefited enormously from the existence of a large pool of private investors who have a natural advantage in information, language, and proximity. No other privatizing country outside the industrial market economies enjoys a similar advantage.

However, despite the existence of a large public sector, Mexico, and Chile (at least before Allende) were market-oriented rather than command economies, with thriving private enterprise sectors. Even Poland and Hungary had small private sectors before the collapse of the command economy during the late 1980s.

CHOICE OF PRIVATIZATION MECHANISM

A comparison of the five countries in Figure 5-1 should dispel the idea that there is a single "best" approach to privatization. For example, the conventional wisdom holds that direct, negotiated sale of a controlling interest to a strategic investor is the most difficult and time-consuming approach, to be reserved for large "flagship" public enterprises and other SOEs of particular strategic importance. However, Germany, Hungary, and Mexico have used the technique of negotiated sale to active investors in order to divest literally thousands of SOEs. (In the case of Hungary, the bulk of the sales have been initiated by the SOEs themselves, with the approval of the government, while in Germany and Mexico the government itself has taken the leading role in the sales.)

The Czech Republic has taken a very different approach to privatization, partly in response to fears that a process of negotiated sales could prove to be too drawn out. As we have discussed, while the Czech approach does not rule out negotiated sales in the case of individual companies, it relies heavily on the use of vouchers. Every citizen is allowed to purchase a book of vouchers at a nominal cost and then to exchange them for shares in companies that are participating in the voucher program or to deposit them in "mutual funds" that invest in such companies. An estimated 2,300 SOEs have been privatized—partially or completely—to date through the Czech voucher program.

Chile's privatization process began in 1974. Until 1984, most Chilean SOEs were divested at auction. Beginning about 1985, the government began selling shares of the remaining large SOEs on the local stock exchange, after offering a percentage of the shares to employees on preferential terms.

Whatever mechanism is used, the key factor appears to be the ability to place large numbers of SOEs up for sale in a short period of time. There is a good deal of truth to the argument that rapid progress in privatization is self-perpetuating; that is, the act of selling a large number of companies at once helps to stimulate an investment climate that attracts additional investors and that creates a demand for additional investment opportunities.

In Czechoslovakia, public interest in the mass privatization program appeared lukewarm until the private investment firm of Harvard Capital & Consulting made its offer (afterwards emulated by many other investment companies) to guarantee a 1000 percent return within one year to private investors who placed their vouchers with HC & C. Almost immediately, public interest in the voucher program soared.

When the Mexican government undertook the privatization of the nation's state-owned banks in 1991, the country's economic recovery was still tenuous, dampening investor interest. Between May 1991 and July 1992, the government sold one bank approximately every three weeks, raising US$12.6 billion in proceeds, which was some 3.3 times book value and 14.7 times earnings.[1] The boldness of the government's action, its timing, and the sheer volume of transactions probably helped to give the bank privatization program a momentum of its own.

LEGAL AND INSTITUTIONAL FACTORS

Legal and institutional factors are important to the extent that they facilitate the rapid sale of a large number of SOEs. Legal and institutional factors that have made a difference in this respect are

- The existence of detailed legal guidelines for privatization
- A unified chain of command for privatization
- Decentralized privatization process
- Sector-specific organization for privatization
- Trained and motivated personnel
- Efficient mechanisms for adjudicating former owners' claims
- Streamlined valuation procedures
- Methods for augmenting low domestic purchasing power

---

[1] Justin Manson, "Mexico: Successful Sale of the Banks," *Privatisation Yearbook 1993*, (London: Privatisation International, 1993), p. 187.

- Ways of shielding investors against "hidden" environmental and other liabilities

Successful privatization programs typically are codified in a privatization law that describes the types of enterprises that are eligible for privatization, which parties can initiate privatization, and the processes and procedures by which privatization can take place. The alternatives are either no law or a law that fails to resolve these questions. The result in either case is the need for time-consuming administrative review or ad hoc approvals of every major privatization project.

The countries that have made the most progress in MLE privatization are those in which a single authority, for example, the privatization agency, is calling most of the shots, without the need to obtain the approval of the Ministry of Finance, the "owner" of the enterprise, or another government entity. For example, the German Treuhand has more power and autonomy than many other Eastern European privatization agencies, although even the Treuhand has to refer questions involving significant financial impacts to a supervisory board or the Ministry of Finance in some cases. The Hungarian State Privatization Agency reportedly also has the final authority to approve most privatizations.

Privatization tends to proceed faster when the process of privatization (as opposed to the authority for privatization) is decentralized. Decentralization can mean either (1) establishing a network of privatization agency offices or (2) giving sellers (either government agencies or the state enterprises themselves) a major role in planning, initiating, and carrying out individual privatizations. In either case, the result is the bypassing of many of the bureaucratic bottlenecks that can hamper the work of the central privatization agency and the transfering of initiative to those who are most familiar with the enterprises to be privatized and are interested in the outcome of the process.

The Treuhand is an example of the first type of decentralization, with its fifteen regional offices. The regional offices relieve some of the administrative burden on the central Treuhand and are closer to the enterprises they are supposed to privatize. They may even introduce an element of competition into the privatization process by competing with the central office for business.[2]

Hungary and Czechoslovakia encourage individual state enterprises to initiate and carry out their own privatization programs, subject to the final approval of the privatization agency. In Hungary, virtually all of the MLE privatizations that have taken place are either "spontaneous" or "self-privatizations." In a spontaneous privatization, the state enterprise transforms itself into a shareholding company, but the transaction is carried out largely by the State Property Agency (SPA). In a self-privatization, the enterprise engages a consultant to assist it in the transaction, which is subject only to the SPA's final approval.

In addition to decentralizing the decision-making process, it is also advantageous for the privatization agency to organize at least partly along sectoral lines, since privatization strategy is, to a large extent, sector or even industry-specific.

Once again, the Treuhand is a useful example. The Treuhand is organized under six board directors who are responsible for specific industry sectors, each of whom has knowledge about and a database for the sector, as well as its own sales and marketing functions. The Hungarian State Property Agency also is in the process of moving from a functional to a more sector-specific organizational model.

The decentralized approach to privatization, in particular, is likely to succeed only if the branch agency or enterprise

---

[2] Philip Wright, Germany: *A Model for Rapid Privatisation*, in *Privatisation Yearbook* 1991 (London: Privatisation International Ltd, 1992), p. 29.

entrusted with the privatization has the motivation and has been properly trained to carry out its task. The staff of many privatization agencies are career bureaucrats, many of whom spent the first part of their careers under the old Socialist system. At worst, they may be unsympathetic to the aims of privatization; at best, they are civil servants who generally are not held accountable for the speed of change.

The Treuhand has tried the innovative approach of employing a substantial number of German businesspeople on its staff. Their pragmatic outlook has been given much of the credit for the agency's simple, direct approach to privatization, which relies primarily on direct sales rather than elaborate schemes involving public flotations or the use of vouchers. Their approach may also have been dictated, to some extent, by the rapid deterioration of East German state enterprises' trading position in the face of West German competition and the introduction of a hard currency.[3]

However, the Treuhand's approach would be much more difficult in most places other than Germany. Not only are experienced businesspeople a much scarcer commodity in most other privatizing countries, especially the former Socialist countries, but also most of the businesspeople who do exist are probably unwilling to sacrifice business opportunities for a much lower-paying temporary civil service career. The fear of possible corruption arising from the misuse of inside information is likely to limit the employment of businesspeople in the privatization agencies, in any case.

OTHER CONTRIBUTING FACTORS

There are other factors that have contributed to rapid privatization. In cases in which state enterprises were created by the nationalization of existing private assets, priva-

---

[3] Ibid., p. 28.

tization may be delayed by previous owners' claims for restitution of their property or compensation. In Chile, the restitution of firms nationalized by the Allende government was relatively fast and easy, because ownership was well established and, in general, significant additions to capital had not been made during the brief Allende period.[4] The delays are most acute in countries such as Germany, where title may be clouded but the law allows previous owners to file claims for restitution, that is, physical return of their property to their ownership.

Ethics aside, compensation is a more pragmatic solution to the obstacle of prior owners' claims than is restitution. In Hungary and Czechoslovakia, former owners are legally entitled only to financial compensation. Compensation, moreover, is linked to the privatization program. In Czechoslovakia, the government retains 3 percent of every firm privatized in order to meet restitution claims. The Hungarian Compensation Bill of 1991 provides for compensation via vouchers, which former owners can use to purchase land or assets that will be privatized.

Governments' natural desire to obtain full value for state companies being privatized should be balanced against the amount of time and effort required to prepare a formal business valuation of every enterprise, particularly in view of the shortage of qualified local valuers in many privatizing countries. In Germany, the Treuhand has tried to streamline the valuation process by valuing companies at the replacement cost of their assets.

One of the purported advantages of the "mass" valuation approach is that it reduces, or at any rate postpones, the need for a painstaking individual valuation of each company. For example, in Czechoslovakia's auction system,

---

[4] Rolf J. Luders, "The Success and Failure of State-Owned Enterprise Divestiture in a Developing Country: The Case of Chile," *Columbia Journal of World Business* (Spring 1993), p. 107.

every share in every company initially is priced the same. The price of unsold shares is lowered in each subsequent auction until they are all sold. Shares that are oversubscribed are not distributed but are offered again at higher prices until a price is found that clears the market.

Low domestic purchasing power is the result of low personal incomes as well as underdeveloped financial institutions. Allowing foreign investment is an important, albeit only partial, solution to the lack of local purchasing power.

Another alternative is to allow generous credit terms to purchasers of SOEs. The experience of Chile between 1975 and 1978 demonstrates the potential dangers of this approach. Since most Chileans lacked significant liquid assets immediately after the Allende period, the government in the early stages of its privatization program sold many enterprises on generous credit terms, with little down payment required. This policy had extremely negative results. Many investors were highly leveraged, which led them to take excessive business risks in order to make the payments on their loans, leading to numerous business failures. Since the enterprises reverted to the government after the investors defaulted on their loans, many enterprises were eventually privatized twice[5]

Governments in other countries, such as Czechoslovakia, are selling vouchers to citizens at heavily discounted prices, which can be exchanged for shares.

Investors may be deterred from investing in some industries, such as chemicals or metallurgy, because they are afraid of incurring "hidden" liabilities for pollution or dangerous or unhealthy working conditions. Governments can address this problem in a number of ways, including reducing the asking price for the enterprise, assuming all or part of the liability (as the Treuhand has done), or setting up a

---

[5] Ibid., p. 108.

fund financed by the proceeds of the privatization program to guarantee investors against hidden liabilities (as Hungary says it plans to do).

SUMMARY

In summary, based on the experience of these five countries, the key factors for success in privatizing medium and large SOEs include a strong domestic economy or, at any rate, one that appears to enjoy favorable, long-term growth prospects. The stronger the local private sector is, the more capital is available to invest in SOEs, and the better the chances are that the overall enabling environment of the country will be favorable to privatization.

No one privatization mechanism (direct sales, auctions, tenders, or voucher privatization) by itself holds the key to rapid progress in privatizing MLEs. What is important is the ability to market a large number of SOEs simultaneously or in a short period of time, fostering confidence in investors that the program is going to work, as well as a fear of being left out if they do not climb aboard the bandwagon.

Whatever privatization approach is used, legal and institutional mechanisms can play an important part in laying the groundwork for rapid progress in privatization. The legal and institutional recipe for success varies according to the conditions in a particular country, but typically includes a strong central authority for privatization, combined with decentralized responsibility for implementing privatization, and a streamlined approach to the task of valuing SOEs.

PART II

A Practical Guide to Privatization for the Investor

CHAPTER 6

Should I Invest In An SOE?

The remainder of this book is intended particularly for investors. In it we will take the prospective investor step-by-step through the entire investment process, from the initial prefeasibility study through negotiating a sale, and on to taking control of the former SOE.

As an investor, the potential advantages of the worldwide trend toward privatization should be apparent to you. In today's global economy, fewer and fewer companies can limit themselves to markets and suppliers in their home countries and hope to remain competitive, much less expand their business. There are over 100 governments— the number increases every year—in every part of the globe, offering to sell or transfer thousands of public enterprises or services, often at distress-sale prices.

The opportunities exist, but there are undeniably risks involved in investing in an SOE. State-owned enterprises, in fact, may not be the most suitable target for every investor. This chapter is not intended to discourage the investor from investing in an SOE, but he or she should enter the process with eyes open. Our intent here is to provide the investor with a kind of "reality check" to ensure that he or she is aware of the risks, as well as the advantages of investing in privatized SOEs and that they are consistent with his or her business objectives before proceeding.

ADVANTAGES OF INVESTING IN A PRIVATIZED SOE

The best SOEs offer important advantages in addition to an attractive price tag. Note the stress on *the best* SOEs. Many SOEs being offered for sale are not commercially viable and are fit only to be closed down and liquidated. (We will return later to the subject of how you identify the good ones.) The better candidates offer advantages such as access to markets, product and technology synergies, lower costs, and other competitive advantages.

Investing in an SOE can help the investor gain access to promising markets in several ways. The most obvious way is by offering a strategic location in or near the target market, or with access to good transport facilities.

Another way is through an SOE's management's knowledge of the market and existing customer relationships. For example, Central and Eastern European SOEs that have traded with the former Soviet Union for years have a network of contacts and knowledge of the market that it would take an investor years to acquire.

Finally, some SOEs enjoy a relatively privileged position in foreign markets by virtue of trade and other agreements between their own country and the market country, such as preferential customs treatment. A special example of an SOE enjoying such preferred status is airport landing rights. One of the reasons that state-owned Central and Eastern European airlines are attractive investment targets, despite their outdated aircraft fleets, is that they have hard-to-get landing rights at congested Western European airports, such as Heathrow.

Some SOEs may help to fill a gap in the investor's product line or may possess technology that will help to improve the overall quality of the products or services offered. A good example of product line synergies is Electrolux's acquisition of Lehel, the Hungarian white-goods manufacturer. Electrolux is known in the West for its high-end vacuum cleaners and other products. The addition of Lehel will give Electrolux a product line that is more suited to Central and Eastern European consumers' financial means and tastes—an important asset for increasing sales to this region.

A U.S. firm, Denver Moscow Associates Inc., formed a partnership with Sibtecom, a Russian high-technology firm owned by Krasnoyarsk State University, in order to introduce and distribute a wide range of Russian technologies in the West, including ceramics, composite materials, thin film coatings, high-temperature coatings, and special treatments for materials to increase corrosion resistance and strength.[1]

Most SOEs—at least those outside the industrial West—have relatively low labor and production costs. In general, these cost advantages, which are based more on market conditions than on superior productivity, are short-term. For example, Manufacture de Sax SA, a French porcelain manufacturer, walked away from the plant it had acquired in eastern Germany after being hit with pay increases of 97 percent in three years. Overall, wage levels in eastern Germany are expected to reach parity with the western part of the country by 1994.[2] Wages in the rest of Central and East-

---

[1] Colorado Company Forms Partnerships for Technology Transfer with Russia," *Eastern Europe Reporter*, Vol. 2, No. 9 (April 27, 1992), p. 358.

[2] "French-Owned Plant in East Germany Shut Down Over Wage, Labor Problems," *Eastern Europe Reporter*, Vol. 3, No. 4 (February 15, 1993), p. 134.

ern Europe are also rising, although not as fast as in Germany.

An investor should not invest unless there is a good indication that the SOE or the country has a long-term comparative advantage. In addition to proximity to markets and low transportation costs (see above), a primary source of competitive advantage in SOEs is access to low-cost and/or high-quality raw materials. Even when a company does not have a direct interest in any of these advantages, it may pay to buy an SOE just to keep it from falling into the hands of a competitor.

The simple fact of having invested in a country, even a small or a peripheral investment, can help local sales by demonstrating good corporate citizenship. On a more substantive level, local partners can help the foreign investor "work the system" in starting and running the business.

EXPLOITING THE ADVANTAGES

Size alone does not determine an investor's ability to exploit these opportunities. Other investors who have gone before include not only the big multinationals but also medium and small businesses and even individual investors. The decision to invest or not to invest should be made based on the specific criteria described below. An investor always has the option of trying to form a joint venture or consortium of investors in order to go after an opportunity if it seems too big to do alone.

The first thing an investor should do is examine the resources available and the overall business strategy in order to determine in general whether, and under what circumstances, acquiring an SOE fits in with that strategy. The investor probably should *not* invest in an SOE if he or she

- Has little or no prior international business experience

- Has trouble financing the acquisition without excessive leverage or robbing from other needed investments

- Expects a quick payback on the investment

- Cannot spare a lot of time or key management and technical personnel from his or her present business

- Is particularly risk averse

Investing in an SOE is one of the most complex transactions that buyers of corporate assets can undertake. In addition to the complications normally encountered in international acquisitions (e.g., political risks, foreign investment regulations, different business cultures), privatizations also may involve the investor deeply in the politics of the host country, with an incompletely defined legal framework to guide him or her, and negotiating partners who are motivated by a very different set of objectives.

Investors can and should hire professional privatization advisers to steer them away from "land mines." However, they should not need advisers to make sure that their business plan reflects an awareness of the general difficulties of doing business in what is, in most cases, a developing country: weak domestic demand for the company's products; underqualified middle management; undermotivated workers; rudimentary distribution channels; and substandard infrastructure, to name but a few. Overcoming these problems requires the patience of Job, a knowledge of what has worked elsewhere, and a lot of cross-cultural sensitivity—all qualities that typically are acquired from years of international business experience.

Risk considerations alone should caution investors against concentrating all of their financial resources in an SOE. Moreover, the SOE probably will be a cash-needer for a number of years. Remember that the money paid for an SOE in most cases goes to the government to be applied to public purposes, such as retiring the national debt, which does not increase the SOE's equity. After the transaction, the investor most likely will have to pay for restructuring costs, working capital, and other financial needs.

The potential returns from investing in a well-chosen SOE can be quite good, particularly in view of the usually low initial purchase price. However, the SOE is likely to be a net consumer of capital for several years, due to restructuring requirements, and the investor may not see any significant returns on the investment for from three to five years or more.

Identifying an investment target and closing a deal may require anywhere from three to five trips to the country. Afterward, some investors find themselves visiting the SOE as often as once a month for the first year, in order to develop a strong personal relationship with management, to assist them in adapting to the investor's own corporate culture, and to smooth out any difficulties with the government and other stakeholders. If the investor does not plan to go to the country, he or she should ask whether one or two senior managers can be spared for that amount of time. The amount of time that a new acquisition will absorb, during and after negotiations, should not be underestimated. If the investor cannot spare the time, it is better to stay away from investing.

RISKS OF INVESTING IN AN SOE

Despite its potential rewards, investing in an SOE involves significant risks and uncertainties. The risks include those risks that afflict virtually every enterprise in a country (such as political or macroeconomic developments, or infrastructure problems), as well as company-specific risks.

In this age of ethnic and national conflicts and "failed nation-states," the investor must choose investment sites with caution. For example, Croatia offers a good location, skilled workers, and some of the most modern factories in Eastern Europe, but the continued fighting in former Yugoslavia scares away all but the most courageous investors. Peru offers attractive investment opportunities, without international conflict, but investors must be concerned with the possibility of a resurgence of Sendero Luminoso-inspired violence that could lead to civil disorder or a military coup. Apart from periodic governmental crises in Russia, the recent local wave of violent crime and extortion from businesses is causing some investors concern about their safety.

Private investors and governments usually make uncomfortable bed partners. Although privatization theoretically means taking the state out of state-owned enterprises, the government often is unwilling or unable to relinquish control completely. In some cases, the government may wish to retain a minority stake in the enterprise. In other cases, the sales contract may commit the private buyer to make certain investments or to employ a certain number of workers, and so on—commitments that may become onerous if the business situation changes. Regulatory mechanisms in many non-Western countries are new, and, as a result, are not sufficiently developed to permit a true arm's-length relationship between government and private business.

Between the possibility of war or civil disorder on the one hand, and heavy-handed government interference on the other, lies the possibility that local politicians will treat privatization as a political football in order to further their own ends, to the detriment of the investment. The country's political leadership may or may not have based its decision to privatize on explicit political considerations but may have unavoidably identified itself with privatization. Opposition parties may oppose the government's privatization program in principle or may use it as a club to beat the government.

Moreover, other groups whose interests are affected by privatization (such as workers) have political connections with the government or opposition groups. As a result, a shift in the political balance can jeopardize the entire privatization process. Perhaps the investor's worst nightmare is a successful repetition of the 1991 Russian coup attempt that nearly brought the Communists back to power. Privatization has been one of the central issues in Russian President Boris Yeltsin's power struggle with the Russian Parliament, culminating in the bloody showdown of September 1993.

Even in relatively stable countries, privatization policy can be subjected to sudden swings. Brazil's privatization program was making progress when President Fernando Collor was ousted for corruption in September 1992. Collor was succeeded by Itamar Franco, who had been a vocal critic of privatization. President Franco imposed a "temporary" moratorium on privatizations. After four months of uncertainty for investors, during which time the head of the privatization program resigned, accusing the president of blocking the program, the program was restarted. In a separate development, the Brazilian Congress announced that it was going to conduct a parliamentary inquiry into sales conducted during the Collor regime. It appears that Brazil's privatization program is now back on track, but the mood of uncertainty acts as a damper on new private investment in state companies.

In addition to the risk that the entire privatization process could be derailed, investors may find that their own investments are uncomfortably in the limelight. For example, there have been instances of a politician or official's trying to embarrass a rival who was closely identified with a particular privatization deal. One tactic is often to charge the official—and, by extension, the investor—with taking bribes and other forms of corruption. The charges are then picked up by the media, which are highly politicized and not hampered by effective libel laws. Although generally not fatal, these tactics can cause the investor considerable embarrassment, not least with the U.S. government, which frowns on such corrupt practices. In most cases, privatization takes place as part of an overall process of economic liberalization and reduced government controls. However, the same economic policies that made privatization possible also pose some of the greatest risks.

Since many governments set the price of energy and other inputs artificially low, SOEs have little incentive to adopt the most efficient machinery and production processes. When price controls are relaxed, the price of some inputs increases sharply to approximate world market prices and the industry finds itself uncompetitive.

Many SOEs traditionally have been shielded from the effects of inefficient production and poor product quality by the monopolies they enjoyed in their geographical or product segment. However, liberalization means that other SOEs can intrude on their turf, not to mention the private enterprises that are springing up for the first time. In many cases, the most damaging competition has come from ambitious former SOE employees, who see an opportunity to capitalize on their experience and customer contacts by opening their own business. Some SOEs have lost more than half of their staff to such start-ups.

Even more damaging than the new domestic competition is competition from imports, which are freed from most restrictions in the new economic system. The imported goods often offer vastly superior quality to the domestic article, which tend to lose much of their price advantage as market pricing increases their input costs.

Under the old system, the domestic currency was usually pegged to an artificially high exchange rate. Domestic inflation and dwindling investor confidence lead to increased pressure on the exchange rate so that, when controls are relaxed, the domestic currency usually goes through the floor. The Russian ruble has dropped from Rs. 0.625 to the dollar to Rs. 1,000 to the dollar in just a few years. A weak currency is a mixed blessing: It makes the company's products more competitive against foreign-made goods in export and domestic markets; however, it also raises the cost of imported inputs and contributes to inflation, which reduces domestic buyers' ability to afford the company's products. It also affects the investor's ability to repatriate profits and dividends.

The types of risks just described are "country" risks; that is, they affect all enterprises in the country more or less equally. In addition, the investor must be aware of specific "company" risks that affect individual companies or SOEs, some of which are

- Accounting risk
- Market risk
- Supplier risk
- Labor risk
- Ownership risk
- Liability risk

The lack of Western-style accounting systems can make it difficult to determine the net worth or cost structure of the SOE or to place a value on it. (This is especially true of enterprises in the former Soviet Union and in Central and Eastern Europe.) Extensive work may be required to translate the company's financial statements into a form that is intelligible and meaningful to Western financial analysts.

Cost accounting systems are usually nonexistent. SOEs' financial reporting systems traditionally have been geared mostly to meeting the government's reporting requirements rather than the information needs of management. As a result, it can be extremely difficult to get a true picture of the SOE's operating costs.

The former SOE could lose a key customer or could be shut out of an important market. As mentioned earlier, this could happen because of competition from SOE employees, who have left the company to start their own business and have taken their customer contacts with them. Competition from foreign suppliers under the more liberal trade regime will be especially dangerous as the new owners restructure and strive to improve product quality. (In some cases, the SOE's new owners can obtain a commitment from the government to extend it some protection against imports during the transitional period.) Finally, the SOE's old markets may simply disappear, as market forces drive other SOEs which were its customers out of business.

Bringing quality levels and on-time delivery performance up to the levels demanded by the market is one of the most pressing priorities of most newly privatized SOEs. However, even if the investor succeeds in improving the new company's quality and delivery time standards, he or she remains at the mercy of local suppliers, including other SOEs, over whose quality and delivery times the investor has limited influence. The alternative is importing more inputs from abroad, but the cost of such a strategy may be prohibitive.

In addition to formal and on-the-job training, bringing most managers and workers up to your own standards of performance will involve the investor in the task of remaking their entire job psychology. Many SOE employees have become accustomed to doing a mediocre job in exchange for mediocre pay and working conditions, plus some valuable fringe benefits (e.g., free housing) and job security. There are plenty of exceptions to this generalization, but, unfortunately, they tend to be the employees who have taken advantage of liberalization to quit their SOEs and start their own businesses. The investor will be trying to instill in those who remain a pride in, and sense of responsibility for, their work and to get them to accept the principle that compensation, promotion, and job longevity should be related to performance. However, some workers, particularly older ones, may not respond to Western-style incentives.

The investor may have to overcome a mistrust of management, which is sometimes a legacy of privatization. In the past, workers wielded a lot of power in many SOEs, especially in the former Socialist countries, and management generally tried to avoid confrontations. Many employees, rightly or wrongly, hold management responsible for the difficulties that their companies were experiencing before privatization. While many employees welcomed privatization (even if they were not prepared to accept all of its implications), others felt that the government and management "sold them down the river." Trade unions, where they exist, do not always play a constructive role in management–employee relations, particularly where more than one union is vying for employees' favor by trying to extract the maximum concessions from management.

Many countries that are privatizing their SOEs are also in the process of adopting Western-style environmental protection regulations. Many SOEs have been serious polluters for years. An investor should find out whether SOEs are "grandfathered" under the new environmental laws or whether the government will assume existing environmental liabilities. If an investor does not do this research, he or she may face large expenditures for environmental cleanup and protection. An investor also needs to be concerned about who is going to be responsible for the SOE's worker's compensation and other employee-welfare programs.

Especially in the post-Communist economies, former owners of nationalized companies now are stepping forward to demand compensation or, in some cases, restitution of their property, which was expropriated by the former government. Different countries deal with restitution claims in various ways, but the investor should be aware that the issue may complicate the selection of an investment target and negotiation of a deal.

Some countries prohibit foreign investors from owning the land on which their plant sits, preferring to grant foreigners a long-term lease. In the case of mineral resources, title usually is not conveyed with the surface rights.

BOX 6-1   CASE STUDY: Risks and the Need for Flexibility in Privatization Ventures

The experiences of the Porex Corporation demonstrate the types of country and company risks that investors run when they invest in SOEs. More importantly, the company's preparedness and resourcefulness show how investors can overcome these risks.

The Porex Corporation is the largest manufacturer of porous tips for pens, as well as a major supplier of specialized medical technology. Germany is one of Porex's biggest markets, and the company's directors were naturally concerned about how German unification would affect business.

Porex found out, through one of its customers in Germany, about a small manufacturing operation outside Bautzen in the former East Germany that produced porous materials and nibs for its parent company, a state-owned manufacturer of writing instruments. Seeing this as an opportunity to gain a presence in Europe, Porex offered to buy the manufacturing operation and to sell part of the output back to the parent company for five years. In addition to supplying the parent company with the inputs that it needed, the deal would furnish a needed cash infusion.

The deal was eventually closed, but Porex soon learned how risky investing in former SOEs can be, especially when the country is making the transition to an open-market economies. One year after the deal was closed, the parent company went bankrupt. Its production costs soared when the German mark was revalued, makings its products uncompetitive. At the same time, it lost the subsidies that had kept even unprofitable companies in operation under the old East German government.

The bankruptcy cost Porex an estimated $1 million per year in guaranteed sales. Porex was left with an asset that was worth significantly less than it had agreed to pay. Porex proposed to the German privatization agency, the Treuhand, that it renegotiate the deal.

The Treuhand initially was unreceptive to the idea, but, after difficult negotiations, a compromise was worked out. "They (the Treuhand) sold us property, roughly 25,000 square feet, at what was quite a bit below market value," recalls Porex's CEO, Ray Hannah. "We then released them from the balance of that contract. As part of that, we had to agree to put so much capital into the business over five years and increase employment, but those were things we were going to be doing anyway, and we felt if we were going to be there we had to do those things."

Porex had other problems with its new acquisition. "It took a lot of training in quality," Hannah explains, noting that the company was not quality-conscious when Porex took over; it is not really necessary when there is a captive market for the company's goods. Quality controls, systems, and procedures, as well as the training required to monitor such controls, were required when Porex stepped in.

Hannah says that the employees were technically already very good but spoke virtually no English. A little bit of cross-cultural orientation and English-German lessons made this situation tolerable. Fortunately, as well, someone in Porex's American accounting office is a native German, and she has been able to work with the employees in Germany. This was fortuitous, considering that, in Hannah's words, "There is almost no knowledge of accounting in that part of the world at all."

Whereas productivity was a foreign concept to workers when their company was owned by the state, workers now recognize that they and the company as a whole benefit as a result of increased efficiency and productivity. Timing is important. After production and efficiency began to increase, the new owners familiarized the employees with good old capitalist work ethics and incentives, and the result, as mentioned, has been very rewarding indeed.

One thing that no one at Porex had anticipated and no amount of legal, accounting, or other professional assistance could help with was the abysmal lack of infrastructure in East Germany. "You could not get a phone call out of there," Hannah recalls, still sounding a little exasperated. "You could get a phone call in from

America, but they could not phone us, sometimes for days on end. That has been resolved. We could not get supplies and had to ship things like nuts and bolts from here because there were just no industrial supply houses around. Those things now have changed so I would say that, by now, 75 percent of their needs they can buy locally. But for the first year to the first year and a half, it was a very difficult situation. But we were able to cope with it, and it worked out all right."

In spite of all the difficulties, Porex's investment in privatization already seems to be paying off. In addition to helping the company expand its writing instrument business, the company is also beginning to identify markets and potential clients for its medical technology products. Regarding overall production, Hannah says that productivity doubled in the first two months and that the firm actually made a profit in the first nine months of operation.

STRATEGIES FOR MINIMIZING RISK

As discussed in Chapter 2, forming a joint venture with an SOE instead of making an equity investment is one way of limiting risk. Another alternative to investing in an SOE is making a "greenfield" investment (i.e., building a completely new facility). In some countries, such as Germany, there may also be private companies that are attractive candidates for acquisition or a joint-venture partnership. A brief discussion of the pros and cons of each approach, compared with equity investment in an SOE, follows.

Forming a joint venture with an SOE is really a particular form of privatization. However, although the state and the private investor, in effect, become joint shareholders, there is no commingling of assets. In most cases, the private partner's risk exposure is less than in an equity joint venture. The overall investment is usually smaller and may be partly outside the country's borders, for example, a foreign distribution network. If push comes to shove, it is easier to walk away from a joint venture than an equity investment. It is

noteworthy that in Russia, where the risks of direct investment in SOEs are perceived to be huge, joint ventures are
extremely popular among foreign investors, whereas direct
investments are almost nonexistent.

The downside of most joint ventures is that the foreign
partner usually has less control over key business decisions.
Decisions are made jointly with the SOE partner, which may
have its own interests and objectives. Many joint ventures
commit the foreign partner to supply equipment, technology,
and/or know-how. However, it may be difficult to achieve the
expected improvements in productivity and quality if the personnel who will operate the equipment or use the technology
and know-how remain employees of the SOE.

"Greenfield" investment allows investors to design and
structure the business according to their needs and those of
the market, instead of spending money on outdated or
inappropriate technology, machinery, and facilities, and
involving them in all of the messy restructuring issues necessary in most privatizations. Indeed, there may be no alternative to making a greenfield investment if candidate SOEs
cannot be restructured economically. Hidden liabilities,
such as the cost of cleaning up past environmental abuses,
by definition are not a problem. All of the money goes into
the business, rather than the government's pocket. The
investor can hire the most qualified and motivated local
managers and employees, in the numbers needed to run
the business efficiently. The investor can also look at what is
not working for competing companies in the region and try
to learn from their mistakes and improve on the way they
are running their operations.

However, the cost of building a company from scratch is
usually several times higher than that of acquiring an SOE,
although, as we have noted, all of the greenfield investor's
money goes into the enterprise, rather than a large share of
it to the government. The greenfield investor also avoids

the problem of valuing the SOE's assets. The investor may find it difficult to find a suitable site for the business, that is, a site that is accessible to markets and/or suppliers and that has the required infrastructure. (Some countries, such as Albania, ban foreigners from owning land altogether.) Some other investor(s) may acquire an SOE and succeed in restructuring it into a strong competitor.

Investing in a local private company has the practical drawback that, in many post-Socialist and developing countries, there are almost no private enterprises worth investing in. The government has dominated the economic life of these countries, often for decades. Most investment has gone into building up the SOEs, which often have enjoyed monopoly status. In most cases, private enterprises, if they do exist, are rather marginal.

Where local private enterprises that are candidates for investment exist, the principle is very much caveat emptor. Since the owners have an interest in obtaining the highest price possible for their company, and standardized accounting and disclosure practices hardly exist, researching potential acquisitions is both important and extremely difficult. In the end, the typical private company is subject to many of the same country and company risks as an SOE, including the risk of market dislocations, competition from imports or new market entrants, problems with suppliers, and a weakening currency.

This chapter has tried to provide you with an overview of the advantages, as well as the potential difficulties, of acquiring an SOE. The initial decision to proceed must be yours. If the difficulties and risks seem imposing, the potential rewards are there as well. Remember also that many other investors have traveled the same route, and by now there is a large body of experience in dealing with them. You may also wish to retain expert advisers to help you resolve the thorniest issues (see Chapter 11).

CHAPTER 7

What Country Should I Invest In?

This chapter has two objectives. The first is to enable you to narrow down the search for a suitable investment target to manageable proportions while making sure that you take into consideration all of the strategic possibilities offered by privatization. The second is to help you assess the advantages, as well as the risks, of investing in a particular country before you make a long-term commitment.

You probably have a specific country or countries in mind for your SOE investment. However, we recommend that you evaluate all of the realistic alternative locations before you make a final choice. We know of one investor who went through a year-long courtship with an SOE in Eastern Europe, only to wind up looking for a joint venture in China after the original deal soured. It might have saved a lot of time and money if the investor had started by looking at all of the alternatives.

This chapter will help you to develop a "short list" of possible countries (and, in the case of large countries like Russia, regions within the country), based on general country screening criteria that do not involve much detailed research to apply. It also gives you a checklist of more in-depth factors to consider when you are evaluating a particular country as a potential investment site once you have identified one or more target SOEs.

DEVELOPING A "SHORT LIST" OF POSSIBLE INVESTMENT SITES

In developing your "short list," you should not attach too much significance to the fact that a country has an SOE in your target industry *per se*. The decision to locate an SOE in a particular country or region may not have been made for rational economic reasons at all, or, at any rate, it may not have been made for the same economic reasons you would take into account in making a decision regarding location. The disastrous economic consequences of this decision may have been obscured by years of input price controls or government subsidies, but they will become apparent when these props are removed. Some of the criteria that have been used to locate an SOE include:

- The "international division of labor"
- Politics
- Employment generation
- Import substitution
- Nationalization of former private assets
- National prestige

The "international division of labor" was a favorite phrase of former Soviet bloc planners. The idea was to combine comparative advantage with economies of scale by building plants large enough to satisfy all, or at least a large share, of the bloc's total demand for a particular product in the country or countries with the greatest comparative advantage in the product's production (such as access to the necessary natural resources).

It is certainly possible to question some of the decisions that were made in the name of the international division of labor, such as the decision to place what was formerly the world's largest forklift manufacturer in Bulgaria, a small market relatively far from the bloc's major industrial centers. The reasons for this decision are obscure but ostensibly were based on the fact that Bulgaria has lots of nickel and zinc, which are used in making the batteries that power electric forklifts.

Politics obviously also play an important role in such decisions ("a factory in every pot"), as well as negotiating leverage ("you support my forklift plant, and you can have your tank factory). Employment generation considerations sometimes motivate the decision to locate an SOE in a particular country or region that lacks sufficient job opportunities for the population.

Import substitution was the goal of many SOEs, especially in developing countries. The idea was to replace imports with locally produced products, saving scarce foreign exchange and providing a springboard for developing exports. However, such decisions too frequently were made without sufficient attention to whether the country had any comparative advantage in these industries. The result was industries that could survive in the home market only with protection against imports and that could never compete internationally.

Nationalization of existing privately owned companies was the origin of many SOEs. In some cases, these companies were established under former colonial rulers with the latter's economic interests in mind rather than those of the country in which they are located.

National prestige is said to be the main goal of some SOEs. National airlines and steel companies of small developing countries often are pointed to as examples of "prestige" projects that never would have been undertaken if business considerations had been paramount.

These are some of the major reasons why, when you start to evaluate different countries as potential locations for your SOE investment, you should go back to the basic questions of what economic, geographical, and other advantages each country offers.

Perhaps you have personal reasons for being interested in a particular country, for example, family or other ties that make you want to participate in its development. Or maybe you are just so bullish on the country's future that you want to get in on the action.

More likely, however, your interest in SOEs is tied to your overall strategic objectives (e.g., increasing profits, penetrating new markets, or maintaining or increasing your share of existing markets) rather than to a specific country. Even if you are initially inclined to invest in a particular country, you should examine your choice in the context of your business or investment strategy, in order to make sure that it meets your business objective better than any of the available alternatives.

Keep an open mind about alternative sites for your investment. Over 100 countries have privatization programs (see Figure 7-1). Obviously, it is neither practical nor necessary for you to analyze all 100 looking for SOEs to buy or to team up with. In the first place, you should be looking at countries that appear to enjoy a potential competitive advantage in the products and markets in which you are interested. In the second place, you should give preference to those countries that provide the most attractive investment environment.

FIGURE 7-1   Countries with privatization programs

**Eastern Europe and the Former
  Soviet Union**
Albania
Azerbaijan
Belarus
Bulgaria
Croatia
Czech Republic
Estonia
Georgia
Hungary
Kazakhstan
Kyrgyzstan
Latvia
Lithuania
Macedonia
Moldavia
Norway
Poland
Romania
Russia
Slovakia
Slovenia
Tadzhikistan
Turkmenistan
Ukraine

Western Europe
Austria
Belgium
Denmark
Finland
France
Germany
Greece
Iceland
Ireland
Italy
Netherlands

Portugal
Spain
Sweden
Turkey
United Kingdom

North America
Canada
Mexico
United States

Latin America and Caribbean
Argentina
Barbados
Bolivia
Brazil
Chile
Colombia
Dominican Republic
Ecuador
Guyana
Honduras
Jamaica
Nicaragua
Panama
Paraguay
Peru
Trinidad and Tobago
Uruguay
Venezuela

Asia
China
Hong Kong
India
Indonesia
Iran
Japan
Malaysia

Pakistan
Philippines
Singapore
South Korea
Sri Lanka
Taiwan
Thailand
Vietnam

Australasia
Australia
New Zealand
Western Samoa

Middle East and North Africa
Algeria
Egypt
Israel
Jordan
Kuwait
Morocco
Qatar
Saudi Arabia
Tunisia

Sub-Saharan Africa
Cameroon
Gambia
Ghana
Guinea
Ivory Coast
Kenya
Liberia
Madagascar
Malawi
Mali
Mauretania
Mozambique
Niger
Nigeria
Rwanda
Senegal
Sierra Leone
Somalia
South Africa
Tanzania

One of the reasons that often is given as justification for seeking an SOE investment is to take advantage of the host country's lower wage structure, or cheap inputs, in order to increase cost competitiveness. The question of why some nations are more competitive than others in particular industries has preoccupied economists since the eighteenth century. There has been a growing realization, however, that low labor and other input costs are not the only influence on competitive advantage—and they are usually a short-term influence at that.

A more complete definition of the factors that help to determine a country's competitive advantage would include the following:

- *Human resources:* Quantity, skill, and cost of personnel (including management)
- *Natural resources:* Arable land, water, mineral, animal, and vegetable resources
- *Geographical resources:* Location, size, and topography
- *Knowledge resources:* Universities and other public and private research institutions, trade and industry associations, databases, libraries, and other repositories
- *Capital resources:* Availability, conditionalities, interest rates
- *Infrastructure:* Transportation, communications

Differences in national economic structures, values, cultures, institutions, and histories also contribute to the way in which nations utilize their resources to build competitiveness.[1]

Theories are fine, but what the potential investor needs is a convenient, straightforward set of criteria for narrowing down the range of countries from which he or she will choose. Some possible criteria include

- Net export position in the relevant product or industry
- A fairly open trade regime
- Access to key markets
- Cultural and linguistic factors

A net export position in the product or industry in which you are interested is a good indication of comparative advantage, especially if exports have been expanding over time.

---

[1] See Michael E. Porter, *The Competitive Advantage of Nations* (New York: The Free Press, 1990).

If the country appears to be self-sufficient in the product or industry in question, you need to look more closely to be sure that domestic producers are not protected by excessively high tariffs or other restrictions on imports. If they are, it is a good indication that they are not competitive. While they may continue to enjoy some protection for a period of time following privatization, you should not count on continued protection over the long term. If the country is a net importer, it is an indication that you should proceed with caution.

The *United Nations Yearbook of International Trade*, which is available in most libraries, is a good source of information on worldwide trade flows. The product groups for which imports and exports are reported are fairly broad, but, if your product or industry is not represented, you can usually find trade statistics for a similar industry.

There are, of course, various other sources of trade data on particular countries or industries. Places to begin your research are the country and industry specialists of the U.S. Department of Commerce in Washington, D.C., or the relevant industry association. However, our purpose at this stage is to help you make a quick identification of the countries that appear to be worth looking at more closely, rather than getting involved in a lengthy research project. Such detailed market research should be deferred if possible until we have identified a candidate SOE.

In some cases, it may be possible to narrow the choice of countries down further, depending on your strategic needs. Start by asking yourself what are the key success factors in your target market (e.g., low delivered price, design features, timely deliveries). For example, the country's location may be an important criterion if inbound and/or outbound transport costs are a significant element in the final price to the customer or if customers require quick delivery. In such cases, you may want to limit the search for

SOEs to countries that are located within a certain radius (e.g., 1,000 km) of a particular reference point. The reference point might be the point of final assembly or fabrication in the case of intermediate goods, or distance from the final market.

Besides physical proximity to your target market, some countries may benefit from lower tariffs or exemption from certain quotas in the target market. If you are planning to ship the SOE's output back to the United States, you will want to focus on countries that enjoy permanent most favored nation (MFN) status, which entitles imports from these countries to the lowest tariffs accorded to any nation. Some Central European states, such as Poland, offer access for some products to the European Community on better terms than other countries enjoy. The Commercial Attaché at the embassy of your target market can give you more specific information on countries that enjoy preferential trading status. Particularly when consumer goods are concerned, investing in an SOE in a country that shares historical, cultural, or linguistic ties with your target market can yield important marketing benefits, particularly insight into local consumer preferences and contacts.

Earlier we recommended that investors who lack significant international experience exercise caution before investing in an SOE. Now we will go even further and recommend that even investors with broad international experience try to stick to countries they know well.

Applying these screening criteria should enable you to narrow down the range of countries significantly, as shown in Figure 7-2.

The country screening criteria described are designed to enable you to narrow the scope of your search for SOEs down to a manageable number of countries, without the need for extensive research. When you have gone one step further and have identified one or more candidate SOEs

FIGURE 7-2 Country screening criteria

Countries with privatization programs

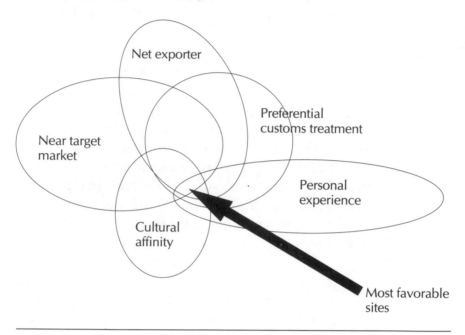

(see Chapter 8), we recommend that you investigate each potential host country's political and economic environment in greater detail in order to evaluate its suitability for your investment as well as any major risks.

EVALUATING THE SUITABILITY OF A PARTICULAR COUNTRY

In the remainder of this chapter, we will describe a number of country evaluation criteria, which require a little more research than the country screening criteria but are designed to help you strike the best balance between the advantages and risks of locating your investment in a particular country. These country evaluation criteria include

- The country's commitment to privatization
- The government's capability of carrying out the sale
- The legal and institutional environment in the country
- Adequacy of the local infrastructure
- The domestic economic conditions

A government may have a privatization program, but, unless it has the political will to carry through on the program, the privatization process may be difficult and even risky. Find out how many privatizations the government has actually carried out. How consistent has the government been over its political lifetime in its support of privatization? Does the government have a pressing need to sell, beyond a general political commitment to privatization? For example, does it have a looming budget deficit that it needs to reduce? Is it under pressure from the IMF or the World Bank to privatize, as a condition for a badly needed loan?

What is the attitude of the major opposition parties toward privatization? Is privatization "above politics," or is it a political issue? How strong is the current government's hold on power? What is the general attitude toward privatization of the government bureaucracies involved?

Even if the government appears to be a motivated seller, it must have the capability to carry out a transaction. Questions to ask include, "Does the privatization agency have cabinet-level status (i.e., does its head have ministerial rank), or is it attached to some other ministry, such as the Ministry of Finance?" Cabinet-level status is an indication that the government attaches a great deal of importance to privatization. Moreover, it means that the agency has the political clout to see its wishes carried out.

What other agencies, if any, must approve the sale (e.g., privatization agency, cabinet, ministry)? The fewer approvals that are required, obviously, the better.

A related question is whether the country has a privatization law that spells out the conditions that must be satisfied and the procedures for privatizing an SOE. In the absence of a privatization law, each privatization must be carried out separately and approved on an ad hoc basis. This is much more time-consuming, obviously, and the likelihood of the deal coming unstuck is much greater.

In many countries, privatization of SOEs is only the first step toward developing a prosperous private sector. These countries lack the laws, institutions, and infrastructure that private enterprise requires in order to survive, much less prosper, that is, the "enabling environment" (see Chapter 1). After years of state control of every facet of the country's economic life, it may be necessary literally to start from scratch in order to develop such an enabling environment.

The best general indicator of a healthy enabling environment is a large and growing private sector. Find out if the country has a history of private enterprise. Does it have a large and/or growing private sector? Other things to check include the following:

- *Legal and regulatory framework:* Does the country have a commercial code and a companies law? Is there a legal framework for resolving business disputes? Do copyright and intellectual property safeguards meet international standards? Can real estate be owned by foreign investors or only leased?

  On another level, is the legal and regulatory framework capable of controlling corruption? Unfortunately, a certain amount of official and business corruption is common in privatizing countries. Corruption can range from "fees" levied unofficially for the processing of documents to demands for protection and threats to the investor's property and personal safety. Uncontrolled corruption can add enormously to the cost and risk of doing business. Participating directly in such corrupt practices is in clear violation of U.S. law, but corruption can affect the investor's business indirectly to the extent that it touches local business associates, customers, and suppliers.

- *Developed banking system and capital markets:* Are the banks and capital markets effective in mobilizing and allocating capital? Even if your investment is financed from abroad, your suppliers, customers, and possibly partners may depend on local sources of financing.

- *Facilitating agents:* Are there facilitating agents, such as bankers, lawyers, accountants, consultants, and similar professionals? The Big Six accounting firms (including Ernst & Young), large law firms, international banks, and consulting firms have opened offices in many of the nations that are privatizing their SOEs. These advisers represent the interests of the Western investor and have established relationships with local firms and professionals who supply the necessary local expertise.

- *Education and research:* Does the country have good technical and vocational education and university-, industry-, or government-sponsored research institutions?

- *Advocacy organizations:* Is there an active Chamber of Commerce or Industry or similar organization that can represent the private sector's interests and opinions with the government?

Everyone has heard the horror stories about infrastructure problems in privatizing countries—phones that don't work, trains that don't run, frequent power outages. Some infrastructure problems are virtually inevitable in most

privatizing countries outside the developed market economies. The point is, will they prevent your investment from
succeeding? Let us take transportation: Maybe the lack of
reliable, efficient transportation is not an insurmountable
problem if your product has long lead times. On the other
hand, if you are in a business in which timely delivery is
critical, such as automobile components, the transport system could make the difference between success and failure.

Alternatively, your estimated investment and projected
returns should reflect the cost of bridging the infrastructure gap yourself, for example, satellite phones, international couriers, even building your own access roads and
operating a fleet of trucks.

You should also determine whether there is a large and/
or growing domestic demand for the SOE's output.
Although we have stressed the significance of a net export
position in a product or industry, do not underestimate the
importance of the domestic market. Worldwide, relatively
few industries or firms have achieved a strong competitive
position by relying on exports alone. A strong domestic
market base also helps to counteract adverse foreign market
or currency trends.

Many privatizing countries are in the process of graduat-
ing from a system of controlled prices to a market pricing
mechanism, sending the price of many inputs into a steep
upward spiral. Caught in the same spiral, customers may be
forced to cut back on purchases. The relaxation of government controls and rapid price inflation frequently also
results in successive devaluations of the national currency,
which makes the SOE's products more affordable to foreign
buyers but increases the cost of imported inputs and makes
profit repatriation problematical. The overall impact is to
increase greatly the risk of investing in a local SOE.

The case of York Luggage's investment in Kofferfabrik
Kindelbruck, a state-owned luggage manufacturer in east-

ern Germany, is a good illustration of the importance of choosing a good location for your SOE investment, although not necessarily in the usual sense.

BOX 7-1 CASE STUDY: The Importance of Location

The York Luggage Company's acquisition of Kofferfabrik Kindelbruck, a state-owned luggage manufacturer located in the eastern zone of Germany, illustrates the contribution that geographical factors can make to the success of an SOE investment. York Luggage is America's third largest luggage company, after Samsonite and American Tourister. Finding itself competing in a relatively depressed market in the United States, York Luggage began to consider expanding globally.

At first, the selection of Kofferfabrik Kindelbruck, which has a dilapidated manufacturing facility in Thuringia, an especially depressed region of eastern Germany, might seem questionable. However, York saw the strategic value in Kindelbruck's location at the geographical center of Europe. With Kindelbruck as a base, York has been able to expand the scope of the company's marketing efforts and to penetrate other European markets.

York consulted with environmental authorities at the federal and regional levels regarding possible environmental liabilities the company might incur if it bought Kofferfabrik. In the end, York had to cover minor deductibles in order to cover the expense of necessary cleanups required as the result of alterations to Kindelbruck. However, because the site was already being used for the manufacture of luggage, relatively few changes to the operation had to be instituted.

The depressed condition of Thuringia has actually been an asset, in an indirect way. The German federal government has spent large sums of money on developing the local infrastructure (including new roads, transportation systems, utilities, and communications facilities) and on training the work force. Despite York's announced plans to cut back employment at Kofferfabrik, York says that it received strong support from local political and business leaders, who view York as Kofferfabrik's—and Kindelbruck's—possible savior.

The country environment is an extremely important determinant of the advantages and risks of investing in a particular SOE. However, the country evaluation should be coupled with a careful evaluation of the target SOE itself, before you make a commitment. The interaction between country and SOE characteristics is the subject of the next chapter.

CHAPTER 8

Choosing the Right Investment Target

Our recommended approach to selecting an SOE has three stages, that is,

- Initial screening of candidate SOEs
- Prefeasibility study, including personal visits to the SOEs
- Detailed feasibility study or "due diligence" analysis

INITIAL SCREENING OF CANDIDATE SOEs

After you have identified one or more promising countries for your prospective investment, the next step is to develop a short list of firms that may meet your strategic requirements. You should begin by contacting the agencies that are responsible for privatization in each of your target countries. A partial list is found in Appendix C; for other countries consult the local U.S. Commercial Attaché's office. Ask them for a listing, with general descriptions, of the SOEs in your target industry or business that are expected to be privatized.

Try to obtain the type of information described below for each SOE candidate. Many privatization agencies publish a brochure that contains much of this information. You can specifically request the rest of the information by fax, telex, or letter. The quality and timeliness of the privatization agency's response should tell you something useful about how well motivated and organized it is.

If the privatization agency cannot supply this information, try the local U.S. Commercial Attaché's office. Most of this information should be obtainable easily for the majority of SOEs, and it will tell you quite a lot about each company, that is,

- *Name/address of company:* Note the location on a map of the country or region. Unless the company is involved in natural resource extraction or processing or the agricultural sector, a location distant from major industrial or population centers raises the possibility that it was established to fulfill a noncommercial policy aim of the government, such as employment generation.

- *Names and addresses of parent company or subsidiaries, if any:* Is the company highly integrated (vertically or horizontally)? If so, it is likely to require time-consuming and potentially expensive restructuring to make it commercially viable. SOEs, particularly those in former Socialist countries, tend to be much more integrated than commercial enterprises. The tendency toward vertical integration reflects the problems that SOEs have had with suppliers, which has led many of them to establish their own in-house sources of supply, even when they do not appear to be commercially justified. Often, enterprises that share little or nothing in terms of technologies or markets are grouped into a single mega-SOE, or *kombinat,* with the inefficiencies and loss of management focus that you would expect from such an organization.

- *Form of organization:* Is the company organized as a joint stock company, with the state holding all of the shares at present, or is its reorganization as such pending? Normally, this is the first stage on the road to privatization. If the company has not been reorganized yet as a joint stock company, it is likely to result in delays in the privatization process.

- *Date facilities were constructed/modernized:* A recent date of construction or modernization is an indication that the technology used is relatively up to date and in serviceable condition.

- *Name and nationality of designer:* A well-known Western designer is another sign that the facility may not require substantial improvement to place it on a commercial footing.

- *Nationalization or government start-up:* How did the SOE come to be in state hands? Was it established by private investors and subsequently nationalized, or was it conceived and set up by the state? This factor cuts two ways. On the one hand, a company that was nationalized is more likely to be subject to claims for restitution, in countries whose laws allow such claims. On the other hand, if private investors started the company, it may be an indication that it enjoys some comparative advantage.

- *Employment:* How many employees does the SOE have? Compare the company's ratio of employees to sales with the ratio for an American or Western European company in the same or a similar industry, in order to get a rough indication of the degree of overemployment in the SOE. The greater the degree of overemployment is, the more pressure there will be for politically difficult and potentially costly restructuring.

- *Operating performance:* Has the company consistently generated an operating surplus, or have government subsidies been required to cover losses on operations?

- *Export experience.* It is an extremely favorable sign if the company has had significant hard-currency exports, indicating its ability to compete in a market environment. Do not attach too much significance to the exports of SOEs that are located in former Socialist countries to other former Socialist countries.[1]

- *Market share:* You may not be able to get this information from secondary sources, but a reasonable market share (say, in the 15–30 percent range) is an indication that the SOE has been able to hold its own in a competitive market. A very large market share (50 percent or larger) is not necessarily a good sign, because it indicates that the SOE enjoys government protection or even quasi-monopoly status.

---

[1] Until 1990, trade among the former Socialist countries was conducted within the framework of the Council for Mutual Economic Assistance (CMEA). Member governments concluded annual trade agreements in which they undertook to buy specified quantities of certain goods from each other. These transactions, which were not valued at market prices, were supposed to be mutually offsetting, so that no country would have a trade deficit at the end of the year. In fact, some countries (notably the USSR) had difficulty producing enough goods that anyone else wanted, so they accumulated large deficits vis-à-vis their CMEA partners. This situation, along with the end of Soviet hegemony in Central and Eastern Europe, led to the demise of the CMEA in the early 1990s. Since 1990, exports to former CMEA countries (particularly Poland, Hungary, and Czechoslovakia) have had to compete increasingly with exports from the West. However, a great deal of trade among former CMEA countries is still conducted on a barter or an offset trade basis to conserve scarce hard currency and is not necessarily indicative of true international competitiveness.

- *Infrastructure:* The privatization agency may not volunteer negative information on utilities, transport, and other infrastructure, but the positive information you receive (e.g., access to a nearby airfield or port) may help in screening prospects at this stage.

Use this information to develop a *simple* overall ranking of the SOEs that you are considering. Ideally, you could reduce the evaluation process to a series of yes/no questions for each SOE, as shown in the example in Box 8-1. The objective at this stage is to narrow down the range of potential choices quickly, without the need for time-consuming research and analysis. A sample evaluation format is provided in Box 8-1.

BOX 8-1   Sample SOE ranking format

The example below shows how you can use the information that you have gathered to identify the best SOE prospects for further investigation. Essentially, it poses a series of yes or no questions, to which you can assign a numerical response (i.e., yes = 1, no = −1, don't know = 0). The responses are added to obtain a cumulative score for each SOE.

Of course, you can take a more sophisticated approach, depending on your needs and the amount of data you have available. For example, you might add weighting factors to stress the criteria that are most important in the light of your overall strategy. However, we advise you not to take an unnecessarily complicated approach. The objective at this stage is to limit the range of choices to the most promising candidates as quickly and expeditiously as possible.

	SOE 1	SOE 2	SOE 3
Strategic location?	1	1	−1
Not an integrated producer?	−1	1	1
Formed through nationalization?	0	1	−1
Joint stock company?	1	1	−1

Built/modernized last 5 yrs.?	0	−1	1
Western technology?	1	1	1
Market share 15–30%	0	1	−1
Hard-currency exports?	1	1	−1
Employment/output ratio?	−1	−1	−1
Operating profit?	−1	1	0
Access to required infrastructure?	1	1	−1
Total	2	7	−4

The example evaluates three hypothetical SOEs. SOE 2 appears to be the most attractive candidate overall. It is strategically located near a major market, and enjoys convenient access to rail and sea-port facilities. Its former private owners undoubtedly perceived the location's strategic value when they established the company, which was subsequently nationalized. However, the founders' heirs do not have any legal claims to restitution, since the laws of the country prescribe that former owners should be compensated for their claims out of a general fund established for this purpose.

There are indications that SOE 2 has the potential to become an efficient producer. The plant was built more than five years ago, but uses efficient, if not state-of-the-art technology. Due to over-employment, average productivity is on the low side, but due to low wages, this has not prevented the company from capturing a large share of the domestic market and even making some export sales to the demanding Western European market. The company has been operating in the black for the past several years. SOE 2 has already been converted into a joint stock company under the country's new companies law, which will expedite its privatization.

SOE 1, like SOE 2, has a good location, employs Western technology, and is a successful exporter to hard-currency markets. However, it has several parts-making subsidiaries that are causing the company to lose money. Overall, it has some promise, but it is not as immediately attractive a candidate as SOE 2.

SOE 3 is even more troubled. It was built near an outlying city, far from its major markets or even a major transportation artery. The previous government decided to have it built there, report-edly to assure the local political boss' support. This is too bad, because it is a relatively new plant and employs modern Western technology. However, it has trouble competing in domestic as well as foreign markets, due to the difficulty and expense of getting products to market, and so it has been losing a lot of money.

SITE VISITS

Before deciding which SOE is your primary target, you should make a personal visit to the three or four top-ranked SOEs on your list. This initial visit gives both sides a chance to size each other up and to determine whether the relationship is likely to succeed.

You, as the key investment decision maker, should go in person, if possible. If you do not have a technical background, take one of your managers who has. Your counterparts on the SOE management team probably have no experience running a market-oriented business. On the other hand, they probably have good technical training in the industry, and thus this is the only framework they will have for evaluating you as a potential partner.

Remember, you are there to do more than "kick the tires," although obviously you should see the facilities, talk to supervisors, and even chat with a few of the workers. Engage management in a frank discussion of what they think are the main opportunities and challenges facing their company under the market economy, such as

- *What is the SOE's long-term strategy?* Do not be too surprised if its management have trouble answering this one. If they respond, it will very likely be with sales objectives (e.g., protect our market share, or double sales within three years). Remember that they come from a system in which a state enterprise is probably judged primarily by its ability to achieve quantitative output targets. Because they enjoyed a virtual monopoly over the market and/or the product usually was in short supply, selling it was never a problem.

- *How does privatization fit into this strategy?* Has the SOE submitted a privatization proposal to the government? (Some countries permit individual SOEs to propose a plan for their own privatization.) What role does it envision for foreign private investment?

- *Who has to sign off on the privatization plan (officially or unofficially), in addition to the privatization agency?* For example, does the municipal government have to give clearance? At this stage, knowing all the interested parties will give you a sense of how complex the negotiations to buy the SOE are likely to be. If you later decide to go ahead with the investment, it will be essential to secure the consent—or at least the acquiescence—of all interested parties. This can be quite a complex proposition, as shown by the case study in Box 8-2.

BOX 8-2   CASE STUDY: Multiple Stakeholders

The government of a South American country has decided to privatize a domestic passenger airline operated by the Air Force, but it must obtain the approval of diverse stakeholders before it decides on the form that privatization will take. These stakeholders include

- The Ministry of Transport, which is in the process of developing a national aviation policy and which does not wish to see its decision regarding the airline's future role preempted by the privatization agency

- The Air Force, which "owns" the airline and generates a significant cash income from its operation, not to mention the opportunity it gives for training air crews

- Local governments and residents of remote areas, who worry that privatization will lead to the curtailment or termination of local air service

- Several competing private airlines, which have complained about government competition in the past and are now jockeying to take advantage of the military airline's privatization

- *How qualified is current SOE management?* Try to meet with all of the company's top managers and form an impression about their abilities. There is a great deal of variation in the quality of SOE management. The older managers tend to have an engineering or technical background and little experience in running a market-oriented business. In the years before and immediately after the overthrow of the old regime in the former Socialist countries, you could assume that most of the upper-echelon SOE managers had strong party connections but that more and more of them are being replaced, especially outside the former Soviet Union.

  There is a shortage of qualified replacements, however, and many of the new appointees are hardly more qualified than their predecessors. These individuals were appointed because of their connections with the new government. They know little about the business and appear to be motivated chiefly by personal political and/or financial advantage. However, because of their political importance, they can be a force to be reckoned with.

- *What long-term role does SOE management see for itself?* Do top managers see themselves as caretakers, content to preside over the transition to a market economy and then leave gracefully? Or do they see themselves as part of the company's future and are even interested in buying a share (or all) of the company? Management's long-term commitment to the future of the company could be seen as a plus, if they have the necessary qualifications and you can work together. On the negative side, they may resist you, if you try to appoint your own personnel choices to key posts. They may even compete with you for ownership of the company.

- *What are the SOE's major markets?* Are they growing, mature, or declining? Are there any identifiable market niches this company could help you fill? Do you know anything about selling these products or markets?

- *What are the SOE's strengths and weaknesses?* Do they complement, or mirror, your own company's? Is there a synergy between the two companies?

- *How much investment will be required to exploit the SOE's strengths and correct the weaknesses?*

- *Basic product technology/processes.* Is the basic technology consistent with that used in your company?

- *Is the SOE liquid?* Can the company pay its current bills? Is it facing a cash crisis, which could shut it down before it has a chance to go private?

- *How much of the SOE's operating revenues go toward debt service?*

- *Does the SOE have significant nonproducing assets, such as worker housing and recreation facilities?* In addition to producing goods or services, many state-owned enterprises (particularly in the former socialist countries) historically have provided employees with a wide range of social benefits such as subsidized housing, recreation, and meals. The assets used to provide these social services do not contribute directly to the company's bottom line, and managing them may be a significant burden on management. Often, these assets are separated from the SOE before privatization, and sold either to employees (particularly in the case of housing) or private investers (as in the case of restaurants and vacation resorts).

- *Are labor relations good?* Securing the cooperation or at least the acquiescence of the SOE's workforce will be one of the new owner's most important tasks after privatization, not only where difficult decisions such as layoffs are concerned, but also in improving quality control and other operational areas. Specifically, are SOE employees unionized? What union(s) represent(s) them? What is the rank-and-file's attitude toward privatization? If given the chance, would employees like to buy all or a percentage of the company? Do employees expect to have a say in the privatization?

- *Are there restitution claims?* Are there any known claims by previous owners? What is the deadline for claimants to make their claims known?

- *Are there environmental problems?* Is the company in compliance with existing environmental laws? What steps have been taken to make sure that it complies with future, more stringent laws?

Before you leave the country, meet with the officials of the privatization agency, as well as other major decision makers and constituents (such as the municipality). Specific issues that you should explore with them include the following:

- *Timetable:* What is their target date for privatizing the SOE?

- *Procedures:* Is the government open to the idea of a negotiated sale, or does it intend to use another procedure? (See Chapter 2.)

- *Conditionalities:* What conditions do the government and other stakeholders expect to place on the deal, such as the number of workers who must be retained or the amount of money the buyer must invest in the company?

- *Debt cancellation:* Is the government prepared to cancel all or part of the SOE's debts as part of the deal?
- *Other liabilities:* Will the buyer be responsible for funding former SOE employees' pensions? Is the government willing to indemnify the buyer against environmental liabilities resulting from SOE practices?

Use the data that you have collected in the site visits, together with additional data on country risk factors (see Chapter 7), to select the SOE you intend to investigate further. The weight you assign to different factors will vary according to your own objectives and business situation but will generally include the following:

- *Ease and speed* with which privatization is expected to take place, taking particular account of the conditionalities that the government or the investor intends to attach, and the number of stakeholders to be dealt with
- *Synergies* between your company and the SOE with respect to strategies, markets, products, and/or technology
- *Amount of restructuring* required, compared with potential returns
- *Debts and liabilities* of the SOE

FEASIBILITY STUDY OR "DUE DILIGENCE" ANALYSIS

The final stage in the selection process is the preparation of a detailed feasibility study. The basic aim of the feasibility study or "due diligence" analysis is to verify that your proposed SOE investment is financially viable or, in somewhat more technical terms, that the projected returns from your investment are both higher than your cost of capital and better than those available from any available alternative investment (taking risk into account).

In some cases, particularly larger SOEs, the government and its advisers may have prepared an information memorandum that presents much of the required information. While the availability of an information memorandum simplifies the task of data collection somewhat, it is still up to you to verify the memorandum's principal findings and conclusions through your own "due diligence" analysis. In either case, you should give special attention to the following areas:

- Market projections
- Financial structure of the company
- Valuation
- Discount rates

Market projections are fairly straightforward if you plan to convert the SOE to producing inputs for your existing product line or to producing carbon copies of your products to sell in geographic markets in which your company already is present. You probably have a pretty good idea of size and nature of the market already.

Sales projections are more problematic if the SOE is to continue producing its existing product line or an upgraded version of it. Increasing international competition, especially from low-cost, high-quality Asian producers, has rendered many SOEs' products virtually unmarketable, because of quality or design deficiencies. In these cases, usually your only chance is to try to find a market niche in which the SOE's product still meets an important customer need. The classic example of this strategy remains the introduction of the Yugoslavian-made Zastva car into the United States as the "Yugo" in the 1980s. The Yugo was technically outdated and lacked many of the amenities that American car-buyers typically expect, but, because of its low price, it found a willing market among buyers suffering from "sticker shock." The Yugo venture eventually collapsed, but for reasons that had more to do with after-sales service than the original marketing concept, which verged on the brilliant.

You should also be particularly careful in your market projections if you plan to use the SOE as a springboard to produce and/or market your products in new markets, particularly in the former Soviet republics. Lack of data and the essential volatility of these markets make risky any projections of future sales volume. Your price assumptions may also prove tenuous as the uncertain market forces you to make pricing concessions or to adopt unconventional payment mechanisms, such as offset trading arrangements.

This is the stage at which you must finally come to grips with the SOE's financial statements. The main objectives are to determine, as accurately as possible, what the cost structure of the company is and what are its assets and liabilities. The results will indicate the SOE's short-term liquidity, potential cost competitiveness, and problem areas that must be dealt with, and will provide major inputs into the valuation process.

The financial analysis can be, and often is, a frustrating exercise. Particularly in the former Socialist countries, the company's financial statements first must be transformed according to Western-style generally accepted accounting practices (GAAP) in order to be intelligible. Even after they have been transformed, it can require substantial educated guesswork to deduce what its cost structure is. Particularly in the developing countries, these problems often are compounded by inaccurate or incomplete data on key cost elements.

The standard practice among many privatizing governments is to value an SOE at the book value of its assets (i.e., purchase cost less depreciation, sometimes adjusted for inflation to yield a "current market" value). The results may be way out of line with the SOE's actual value to an investor, particularly if the SOE's assets or its product line are outdated.

We recommend that investors have the SOE valued by a professional valuation expert. If the company is not operating, the assets should be valued at their fair market value, that is, the price of similar assets being bought and sold separately on the open market.

In the case of an operating company, the best approach is usually to perform a "business valuation." In a business valuation, the company's future cash flows are projected five or ten years into the future and then are discounted to reflect the investor's cost of capital or perceived risks.

Where possible, the results of the business valuation also should be compared with the price paid for other companies that have come on the market in the last few years and that have roughly the same size and strategic situation. This kind of comparison is particularly useful if the assets have a strategic value to the investor that is not reflected in the SOE's historical sales performance. A good example is a state-run Eastern European airline, whose assets may consist of beat-up Soviet aircraft with little residual market value and whose operating losses may have required massive state subsidies to keep it flying. Nevertheless, if the airline has hard-to-get landing rights at crowded airports, such as Heathrow, it may be be able to command a relatively high price because of its strategic value.

In our discussion of business valuations, we mentioned the discount rate as a key determinant of the SOE's value.

The discount rate corresponds to the annual rate of return that the investor would like to receive on the SOE invest-ment, considering cost of capital, the rate of inflation in the country of investment, and the level of risk that he or she is incurring.

A technical discussion of discount rates is beyond the scope of this book. Again, we recommend that you hire a valuation professional for this part of your acquisition anal-ysis. However, you should be aware that the discount rate for SOE investments frequently is extremely high by West-ern standards—sometimes exceeding 20 or even 30 per-cent. As a consequence, the price paid for the SOE usually must be a real bargain in order to justify the investment.

Let us assume now that you have chosen your target SOE and that it looks like a good investment, provided you can get it for the right price. In the next chapter, we will discuss different approaches for making an offer to the host gov-ernment and for negotiating a deal.

CHAPTER 9

Negotiating A Deal

Having decided to try to invest in a particular SOE, you may be wondering what, exactly, you have gotten yourself into. There is no simple answer, because the privatization process varies a great deal from country to country, and even from transaction to transaction within a particular country.

INVESTMENT MECHANISMS

Among the privatization mechanisms described in Chapter 3, there are four basic avenues (with local variations) for a foreign investor to take when acquiring an equity stake in an SOE. In some cases, more than one avenue is taken in a particular country; in other countries, the law prescribes one avenue. The four avenues are

1. *Direct sale.* The investor negotiates directly with the government for up to 100 percent of the company.

2. *Tender.* Sealed bids for the company are solicited from interested parties. The bids are opened on a set date, with the company going to the highest bidder.

3. *Financial market mechanisms.* Shares in the company are offered on local and, in some cases, foreign stock markets.

4. *Voucher ("mass") privatization.* Voucher privatization is a technique that has been pioneered in some post-Socialist countries as a way of distributing ownership to their citizens. In these countries, every eligible citizen receives a voucher or vouchers either gratis or for a nominal fee. These vouchers can be exchanged for shares in SOEs or for mutual funds that invest in SOEs, or can be traded in the secondary market. Voucher privatization is not of great interest to foreigners in most cases, with the major exception of Russia. In Russia, vouchers acquired in the secondary market are the primary avenue for foreign investors to acquire ownership shares in former SOEs.

A variation on the tender arrangement, which has been used with considerable success, particularly in Argentina and Chile, is the debt-equity swap. With the government's agreement, the investor buys government debt in the international financial markets at a discount. The government then redeems the debt at face value or an agreed-upon percentage of face value, and the investor puts the proceeds toward the purchase price of the SOE.

As also noted in Chapter 3, an estimated 90 percent of all privatizations in the industrial market economies have been direct sales or public share offerings. In other countries, most larger firms have been privatized through direct negotiations, tenders, joint ventures, or the sale of a core shareholding to a strategic investor. Public share offerings are not used nearly as widely in the former Socialist and developing countries, because their capital markets tend to be underdeveloped and most SOEs are in poor shape.

Normally, the investor does not have a voice in determining which avenue is to be taken. However, the various avenues offer different advantages and drawbacks from the investor's standpoint:

- *Ease of implementation:* A tender is probably the quickest avenue to take in order to acquire an interest in an SOE. A direct sale, on the other hand, can involve months or even years of detailed negotiations. (See Box 9-1.) Voucher privatization is probably the most difficult avenue for a foreign investor to take. This is one of the main reasons why foreign investors have shown little interest in acquiring Russian SOEs, preferring to go the joint venture route instead.

- *Lowest price:* A negotiated sale usually results in the lowest price paid, because of the lack of competition. However, a tender in which part of the bid price is paid in debt instruments (debt-equity swap) can also result in a very good price.

- *Transparency:* A "transparent" transaction is one in which there is the least possibility, and therefore the least suspicion, of improper practices or corruption. As we discussed earlier, the privatization process can become highly charged politically, with various interests accusing one another of corruption to secure a political advantage. The foreign investor has no interest in getting caught in the crossfire. The attractiveness of the tender approach may be increased by its transparency.

STRANGE BEDFELLOWS

In the case of some SOEs, you will be allowed to purchase only a partial interest in the company. The government may choose to allocate the remaining shares to different groups—employees, the general public, institutional investors, and the government itself—using various distribution mechanisms.

Often 10 percent or more of the shares are set aside for employees, as a way of increasing their support for privatization and giving them a stake in the enterprise's future. The employee shares often are offered at a discount, and the government may help to finance the purchase. The risk is that these employees, through their representative(s) on the board of directors, will push for higher wages, better benefits, and other concessions. The long-term benefit of employee share ownership is that it tends to motivate employees by linking their dividend income to the company's financial performance.

Additional shares also may be reserved for the general public and institutional investors. The public can purchase shares for cash or vouchers. Institutional investors include banks, insurance companies, as well as the so-called investment funds or mutual funds that have been set up in connection with voucher privatization schemes in some countries. Individual voucher-holders deposit their vouchers in one or more of the funds, which then use them to buy large enough blocks of stock in individual companies to have a direct voice in the management of the companies.

Particularly in strategic industries or in industries whose activities affect the public interest directly, the government may wish to retain a voice on the board of directors, either by retaining a minority shareholding or by means of a "golden share." A golden share is a device by which the government is represented on the board without actually owning any shares. In some cases, the government's right to be represented is limited to certain issues that affect the national interest, such as work force reduction.

Like employee shareholding, continued government ownership of part of the shares or a golden share is a two-edged sword. It can be helpful because it ensures the government's continued attention to issues that affect the company. On the other hand, some investors are fundamentally averse—sometimes for good reason—to sharing control with the government.

It is up to you as the investor to decide whether you find less than 100 percent control, or at least an absolute majority interest, of the company acceptable. In particular, some investors may be uncomfortable with a government voice on the board of directors.

THE ART OF THE DEAL

Let us assume that you have selected the SOE you want to invest in and are about to begin negotiations to purchase a controlling interest in the company. The experience of Basic American Foods in negotiating for a potato processing plant in Poland (Box 9-1) should give you some idea of what to expect.

BOX 9-1   CASE STUDY: Negotiating the Deal

Basic American Foods (BAF) is the biggest potato dehydrator in the United States. Poland is the world's second-largest potato producer, and BAF has been selling potato-processing technology to the Polish government since the 1960s, long before privatization came into vogue. In 1989, the company decided to explore the possibility of establishing overseas production facilities. James Leahy, vice president of BAF's parent company, Basic American Inc., was put in charge of the project.

After investigating a dozen potato-processing plants in Poland, BAF decided to focus on a former state-owned production facility outside Glowno, about 30 kilometers from Warsaw, in the town of Lodz. The next step involved consultations and negotiations with the company about forming a joint venture. "I met with the management a number of times, and we discussed possible ways that we might work together," Leahy recalls. "We talked to the unions and that sort of thing, and tried to explain to the employees what we were thinking about doing."

One major hitch BAF ran into—one that has plagued many investors in the early stages of privatization—was the constantly changing Polish laws on privatization. In the middle of the negotiations, the laws changed in a way that made a joint venture out of the question and that forced BAF to think seriously for the first time about making a direct equity investment in the Polish company.

However, the target company first had to be converted to a joint stock company owned by the Ministry of Finance, as represented by the Ministry of Privatization. A proposal then had to be submitted to the Ministry of Privatization, which was done in December 1991.

According to Leahy, 'When we made our original proposal, the Polish government was positive about everything. I made a point, when I was talking with the fellow from the Ministry of Privatization who was assigned to our particular case, that I understood their need to have legal representation and consultants and that sort of thing. But I said that the negotiations themselves should take place between the principals, as advised by whomever they chose. That didn't happen. I ended up negotiating with a bunch of damn American lawyers!"

The "American lawyers" Leahy referred to were attorneys with a large Chicago law firm that was acting as the official legal adviser to the Polish privatization agency. Both sides were hampered by the fact that legislation governing privatization was just being hammered out and that all parties concerned were, to some extent, unfamiliar with the relevant laws. The American lawyers were on rotation from the United States and were frequently changed throughout the negotiations. Most frustrating of all was the fact that, in 90 percent of the meetings, no one from the Polish government was present. "This probably made the procedure longer and more expensive and frustrating than it needed to be," Leahy says.

As far as the mechanics of the deal go, Leahy says that the members of the Polish government were advertising favors and assistance they were willing to provide investors and privatizers. When it got down to the nuts and bolts of the deal, however, the kind of assistance that had been promoted was not available to BAF during the privatization process. "There was a lack of consistency between (the Polish government's) promotional efforts and what was actually happening." Leahy says that this made it very difficult for him to have to go back to the United States and explain to BAF's owners why they could not receive the kind of assistance that the Polish government had been telling the investment community was available.

For example, the government was telling investors they would not be held responsible for existing environmental liabilities of SOEs that they acquired. "Only after months and months of negotiations afterward did we get anything that even resembled that kind of environmental indemnification," Leahy recalls. The entire privatization process took BAF about twenty months.

BAF had told the government that it wanted to conclude the deal in time for the annual potato harvest. However, the harvest was well underway before negotiations were completed. "BAF's Polish experience illustrates the headaches—very costly headaches—that can be encountered when privatizing SOEs," says Leahy. "Every business has its peak seasons, and Basic American Foods' had started long before August when the deal with the Polish government was consummated."

BAF bought 80 percent of the shares that were put on the market. The agreements reached during the negotiations included a commitment by BAF to subsequently increase its investment, which had been fulfilled.

The new owners provided the employees with zero interest loans in order to encourage them to buy company shares and thereby have a direct interest in the future of the company. As a result of this, the employees now own the balance of the shares not owned by BAF.

What are some of the lessons we can draw from BAF's experience? Here is a list of some of them.

Be prepared for negotiations to take much longer than you expect. Basic American Foods' experience in Poland makes it clear how important patience and persistence are during negotiations. It has been suggested that you budget at least three times the normal negotiating time and expense for a commercial deal of similar size and scope.[1] You should also have contingency or back-up plans so that delays or complications in negotiations will not jeopardize your overall business objectives.

Pay attention to the personal chemistry of the negotiations. It is widely known that personal chemistry plays a greater role in business negotiations in almost every other country than it does in the United States (especially in the post-Socialist and developing countries), but the point bears repetition here. The highly personal nature of the negotiations is one reason the process takes so long. Many meetings will appear to get nothing accomplished, while your counterparts on the other side attempt to size you up or decide whether they even want to do business with you.

Stay flexible. As BAF found, privatization laws can change at any time, including during the middle of negotiations. Moreover, government negotiators may not be able to deliver on promises regarding incentives for investors. Government policy can change from week to week, and negotiators may not be empowered to make the kinds of decisions you wish they were able to make.

Know who is in authority. You may find yourself negotiating with a changing cast of characters, not all of whom necessarily have the authority to negotiate a deal or who are

---

[1] Thomas M. Blake and Michael S. Blake, "Bear Necessities," *Global Competitor*, Winter 1994, p. 60.

aware of what has been promised by other government negotiators. BAF thought they had a deal on forming a joint venture with the company, only to find that the privatization laws had changed, ruling out such a joint venture.

During negotiations with the government, BAF frequently found itself negotiating with the government's legal representatives, who had no authority to reach agreements on substantive matters. It is important for you to identify who is really in authority and try to exert tactful pressure to move up the negotiating ladder to someone who really is in charge, and then try to maintain contact with that person.

Assign someone to negotiate for you from start to finish. Do not complicate the changing personnel situation on the other side with changes of your own. The person(s) negotiating for you should have the professional stature and authority to command respect as well as to close the deal.

"Get it in writing." As BAF discovered, the investor incentives advertised by the government may not be available when it comes down to hard negotiations. You must ensure that the government can live up to its claims, especially if you have a sizable investment riding on them.

Clarify your liabilities. BAF wisely was willing to negotiate long and hard to get an environmental indemnification clause that it could live with in the contract. Be very sure that you understand your contractual responsibilities for environmental violations that occurred before privatization, including ex post violations under laws passed after privatization.

Another area in which you should be absolutely clear about your responsibilities is your obligation toward the current employees of the company. Are there restrictions on layoffs? For example, the German privatization agency, the Treuhand, places employment clauses in its contracts, with stiff monetary penalties for violations. Who is responsible for financing pensions as well as severance packages?

Make sure you know what you're buying. This problem did not come up in the BAF deal, but you should be alert to it. For instance, some countries do not permit foreign investors to own land, giving them instead a long-term (e.g., ninety-nine-year) leasehold on the underlying real estate. When mineral-related operations are concerned, you should be aware that, unlike the United States, most countries consider subsurface resources to be the inalienable property of the state. What you are buying in such cases is the right to extract the mineral on behalf of the government, which retains the right to make decisions on vital matters such as pricing.

In this chapter, we have tried to give you some idea of what to expect in negotiations. The next chapter is an introduction to what awaits you on day 1 after you have assumed control of your new company.

CHAPTER 10

The Management Challenge

In this chapter, we discuss ways of making sure that your SOE acquisition succeeds and of integrating it into your overall business operation. After reading Chapters 8–11 of this book, does the following sound like a description of a typical SOE?

- Deteriorating sales and market share
- Outmoded product line
- Serious quality problems
- High overall cost of production, largely the result of duplication of activities among divisions and of trying to make too much of the product in-house
- Losing best distributors to the competition
- Bloated management structure, seemingly aloof from what is going on on the shop floor
- Low worker productivity

- Facing major outlays to meet government environmental standards

Well, this is actually a description of one of America's Big Three automakers at its nadir, before a new management team took over, determined to reverse its declining fortunes! The point is that, in many ways, the typical SOE is in a classic turnaround situation.

Turning an SOE around presents certain unique challenges, and they are concentrated in the management area. The following passage was written to describe the situation that existed in Soviet SOEs—and, by extension, other Socialist SOEs—during the mid-1980s. While reforms in the state enterprise system since 1985 have had some beneficial effects, the situation in the post-Socialist countries has not changed substantially. The same remarks also apply generally to SOEs in other countries, particularly those in developing countries.

> The very term "enterprise" was a misnomer. The firms were simply not independent companies, but rather were production units that responded to the directives of superior government offices and decision-makers. Firm directors were much more production engineers than managers. They were concerned first with meeting the physical targets of the plan and second—often a distant second—with the quality of the item produced. Questions of design, cost minimization and the division of retained earnings between rewards for the workers/managers and reserves for the expansion of the firm were not in the control of enterprise management (and the notion of a "dividend"—a return to the owner on the capital invested—was not even considered) . . . [The] enterprises generally operated at low levels of efficiency, produced poor quality goods, mostly failed to maintain high technological standards, and were increasingly producing negative externalities such as pollution."[1]

---

[1] John Nellis, *Improving the Performance of Soviet Enterprises* (Washington, DC: The World Bank, 1991), pp. 2–3.

In other words, it is the management challenge that sets the typical SOE acquisition apart from other turnaround situations. Privatization is the solution to the most fundamental management problem of most SOEs—excessive government control over long-range and day-to-day business decisions—but by itself it does not address management deficiencies in such areas as

- Profit consciousness
- Management training and experience levels
- Strategic planning and marketing skills
- Production planning
- Financial management
- Quality control
- Productivity
- Organizational structure
- Managment information systems

SOE managers are frequently criticized for their lack of attention to the company's profitability. This attitude is the result of both traditional career patterns among SOE managers and the environment in which they must function. The typical SOE manager in many countries either was transferred from the government bureaucracy or military, or else has a technical or engineering background. In either case, executives have had little or no preparation for the rigors of competing in an open market economy.

Until very recently, of course, none of this mattered very much. Executives were judged above all by their ability to match output to plan or other quantitative targets. Operating surpluses, if any, went into the state treasury. The treasury also provided subsidies to cover any operating losses.

Unfortunately, the incentives for capable managers to go to work for state enterprises in most countries have never been great, and they are diminishing in inverse proportion to the growth of the private sector. Management salaries in the private sector are so much higher—up to five times higher than those of SOE managers in some cases[2]—that private enterprise invariably siphons off the best managers. The constant turnover of SOE managers leaving to take jobs in the private sector means that the new managers are forever having to learn their jobs. The lack of qualified, experienced managers is especially severe at the middle management level.

As we suggested in Chapter 8, SOEs typically have no detailed long-range strategic plans. Under the old system, production goals were set by the government. Today, their chief strategic preoccupation tends to be staying solvent long enough to find a private investor. Modern marketing is virtually unknown in SOEs. The "Marketing Department" is usually composed mainly of order takers. There is little or no market research and analysis, outside sales, or customer service.

SOEs tend to be at their best in producing large batches of relatively standardized products. Most of them do not have the production planning capabilities and systems to support flexible manufacturing or products that are manufactured to the buyer's specifications.

Financial management skills, in particular, are in short supply in many SOEs, especially in accounting, budgeting, and cost accounting. Billing control tends to be poor, so there often is a big pileup of receivables. Inventory accounting is a special weakness of many SOEs. There is generally no internal audit function.

---

[2] Mary M. Shirley, *Managing State-Owned Enterprises* (Washington, DC: The World Bank, 1983), p. 48.

Quality control in most SOEs, or what there is of it, tends to be after the fact and not linked to any incentives. There is a lack of preventive quality control, such as sharing the benefits of decreased rejection rates with employees and suppliers through pay incentives.

The issue of overemployment and low average worker productivity in most SOEs is well known. What is perhaps less widely understood is the fact that in many SOEs a significant portion of the overemployment is in the ranks of the middle managers.[3]

The typical SOE is organized along strict hierarchical lines, whose main purpose is the fulfillment of production targets. Decision-making powers tend to be concentrated near the top of the pyramid, rather than decentralized to the appropriate operating levels. Individual operating units do not necessarily have control over the functions necessary to fulfill their responsibilities. It is often difficult to mobilize the resources required for activities that cut across organizational lines, such as new product development.

Most SOEs are characterized by a shortage of internal systems and procedures that would enable them to gather and process information on the external environment and translate it into management decisions affecting operations. Management sets performance targets for the company but has limited means to measure progress toward achieving those goals, to identify potential trouble spots, and to take timely corrective action.

The best approach to meeting the management challenge posed by privatization incorporates a number of basic principles, including:

- Direct, continuing involvement of key managers from the home office

---

[3] Homi J. Kharas, *Restructuring Socialist Industry: Poland's Experience in 1990* (Washington, DC: The World Bank, 1991), p. 28.

- Identifying SOE personnel who have the potential to become effective managers and grooming them to take over management of the company
- Instituting a formal management development program for SOE personnel
- Implementing an incentive system that rewards superior performance
- Installing needed systems and procedures

Plan to bring in one or more of your own key managers for an extended (i.e., at least one to two years) tour of duty with the former SOE, backed up by shorter visits by other managers and technical specialists as required. However, transfers of stateside personnel should be kept to the minimum necessary, because of the cost, as well as the possibility of creating resentment and/or an excessive reliance on outsiders among the SOE staff. You can often minimize such problems by sending in an expatriate manager with local family origins (e.g., a Hungarian-American) who is at least somewhat familiar with the local language and customs.

There are capable and motivated individuals on the management team of almost every SOE who have not had the opportunity to realize their full potential under the constraints imposed by state ownership. Your resident manager should quickly discover who they are and should earmark them for an intensive development program in order to enable them to take over the long-term management of the company.

While earning a Western-style MBA may be the appropriate route for some managers, in general we recommend that you rely on short courses and on-the-job training with counterparts from the home office. A medium-term (e.g., six months to two years) assignment to the home office can accomplish the same purpose, while promoting the absorption of the parent company's corporate culture and the "bonding" or integration of the two firms.

Under state ownership, the most able managers either were thwarted or left the company because of a relatively level pay scale and a career path that rewarded time servers. The obvious defects of this system are magnified when privatization and the general development of the local private sector increases the availability of alternative opportunities. To enable managers to realize their full potential and to protect your investment in developing that potential, you need to find ways of motivating them to superior performance.

Managers need the appropriate tools to help them get their jobs done. Some systems can be imported from the parent company more or less as is, whereas others may need to be tailored or reinvented to suit local business conditions and cultural preferences.

PITFALLS TO AVOID

It may help to review York Luggage's successful acquisition and restructuring of Kofferfabrik Kindelbruck at this point (see Box 7-1). In addition to investing DM4.8 million in Kofferfabrik, York is providing management support, controls, new products, marketing programs, and other assistance in order to make Kindelbruck viable. At the same time, it has reduced Kofferfabrik's work force, which numbered 600 in the company's heyday and which had shrunk from about 130 by the time York bought it to 78. (Current plans are to hire enough workers to bring the total to 100 once sales of Kofferfabrik's revamped product line takes off.) The local and federal governments were understandably concerned about the layoffs but supported York because the company had committed itself to reviving

Kindelbruck, capitalizing it, and training and retraining employees.

However, even the most experienced investor can run into problems in restructuring an acquisition, as the case study of General Electric's investment in a Hungarian SOE shows (see Box 10-1).

BOX 10-1   CASE STUDY: Restructuring Problems

The history of General Electric's investment in the big Hungarian light bulb manufacturer, Tungsram, provides important insights into what can go wrong when a foreign investor tries to restructure an SOE that it has acquired. GE paid US$150 million for a 50 percent share of Tungsram in 1990, as part of a joint venture with the Hungarian Credit Bank and other Hungarian investors.

GE's ads hailed the joint venture's "brilliant future." The deal created the first sizable Western joint venture in the region. Tungsram had been regarded as one of the few truly internationally competitive Hungarian firms, with a 6 percent share of the Western European light bulb market.

By 1992, GE had expanded its stake in Tungsram to 75 percent. Meanwhile, Tungsram's Western European sales (measured in the Hungarian currency, the forint), increased by 50 percent between 1989 and 1992. The number of employees fell from 18,000 to 10,200, and productivity made great strides, rising 14 percent in 1992 alone.

Under GE, Tungsram has withdrawn from peripheral businesses, has halved the number of levels of management, and has cut the turnaround time between order and delivery by 50 percent. GE has made progress in integrating Tungsram with the rest of its worldwide lighting business, establishing four of GE's nine technology centers in Hungary. It appointed a Hungarian executive director of technology for GE Lighting Europe.

Yet Tungsram has been experiencing mounting losses during this period. In 1992, the company lost US$104 million, in its third consecutive year of losses. What went wrong?

Probably the most damaging development has been the continuing appreciation of the Hungarian forint. Coupled with a drop in lighting prices in Tungsram's main export market, Western

Europe, under competitive pressure from archrivals Siemens (Osram) and Phillips, the appreciation in the forint has squeezed profit margins.

At the same time, domestic demand for Tungsram's products in Hungary has remained stagnant because of the local recession. Economic dislocations have also shrunk the company's former markets in Central and Eastern Europe and the former Soviet Union by as much as 90 percent.

Finally, there have been the costs of restructuring, including charges for withdrawing from noncore businesses, accelerated layoffs, a write-off of bad Russian debts, and increased borrowing costs.

In 1993, GE announced that the three years' losses had wiped out the company's equity and that it was recapitalizing Tungsram with an additional investment of US$195 million, bringing GE's total investment to almost US$500 million, and that it would lay off another 900 employees. The company has started an aggressive campaign to get Tungsram's suppliers to reduce prices. The goal is to match the operating margins of Osram and Phillips by 1994, but the company stops short of predicting a return to overall profitability.

The CEO of GE Lighting Europe was put in direct control of Tungsram. GE has stressed that it is in for the long haul, even though it probably underestimated the difficulties that it would encounter with Tungsram. A spokesman has characterized GE's attitude as one of "aggressive patience."[4]

_____

[4] See articles by Nicholas Denton, "Tungsram Fails to Shine for GE," and "GE's Tungsram Posts Third Consecutive Annual Loss," in *Financial Times*, March 17, 1993, p. 45 and March 10, 1993, p. 29, respectively.

What are some of the lessons that we can learn from the experiences of York Luggage and General Electric?

- *Consult with other stakeholders.* The need to coordinate plans with the company's other stakeholders does not end with privatization. One of the reasons York was able to win support for its work force reduction propos-

als was that local leaders understood that it was necessary for the company's—and their community's—long-
term economic well-being.

- *Restructuring alone cannot ensure the investment's success.*
  GE undertook an extensive, and by all accounts successful, restructuring of Tungsram, while Tungsram has
  suffered mounting operating losses. Unfortunately, the
  economic and industrial environment in which GE's
  investment is situated has been counterproductive, at
  least in the short term.

- *Long-term success requires persistence.* When pressed, GE
  spokesmen have admitted that, had it foreseen the difficulties ahead, GE might not have invested so much
  money so quickly in Tungsram.[5] However, GE is cor-
  rectly taking the long-term view and is continuing to
  make needed investments. Of course, not every investor has pockets as deep as General Electric's, which is
  why investors need to determine at the outset whether
  former SOEs are an appropriate investment for them.

The challenges facing any investor, obviously, can be
immense. In the next chapter, we describe some potential
sources of assistance (self-help and outside help) that may
help you in surmounting these hurdles.

---

[5] Nicholas Denton, "GE Faces More Losses at Hungarian Unit," *Financial Times*, September 9, 1992, p. 26.

CHAPTER **11**

Getting Assistance

Various sources of information and even financial assistance are available to investors when they are evaluating and implementing their privatization projects. A number of information sources to help you get started have been mentioned in previous chapters, including the U.S. Department of Commerce country desk officers and the commercial attachés of the embassies of the countries in which you are potentially interested.

FURTHER READING

An extensive list of further readings is included in the Bibliography. As a rule, they provide useful general background on the history and mechanics of privatization in different regions of the world. However, privatization is such a fast-developing field that much of the information they contain, particularly on specific privatizations, is quickly outdated. The following periodicals are among the best sources for information on fast-breaking developments in privatization and leads on specific investment opportunities.

- *Privatisation International*, published monthly by Privatization International Ltd., Suite 510, Butlers Wharf Business Centre, 45 Curlew St., London SEI 2ND, UK (Phone 77-71-378-1620 or Fax 44-71-703-7876). The most comprehensive review of current developments in privatization throughout the world, *PI* is a good source of information on different countries' privatization projects and leads on potential investment opportunities. *PI* also publishes an extremely useful *Privatisation Yearbook*, in which it reviews the previous year's developments in privatization worldwide.

- *International Privatization Update*, a monthly publication of Fin Mark Research Inc., 1576 River Rd., Castleton-on-Hudson, NY 12033 (Phone 518-732-5757). *International Privatization Update* is similar in scope to *Privatisation International*, although the latter generally gives more detailed coverage.

- *Eastern Europe Reporter*, which comes out biweekly, covers privatization developments in Central and Eastern Europe and the former Soviet republics in greater detail than any other publication. Its coverage of general political and economic developments affecting privatization is particularly useful. Potential investors will be particularly interested in the section called "Markets and Deals," which contains interesting descriptions of other investors' experiences. For information, contact the Bureau of National Affairs, Inc., 1231 25th St. NW, Washington, DC 20037 (Phone 202-452-4200).

- *Central European*, in spite of its name, provides detailed coverage of privatization and related developments in Central and Eastern Europe and the former Soviet

Union. Issues of *Central European* contain several feature articles (a recent issue focused on developments in Belarus and Uzbekistan), plus useful regular departments such as "Deals," "Privatization," and "Joint Venture Alert." For information, contact *Central European*, Nestor House, Playhouse Yard, London EC4V 5EX (Phone 44-71-779-8682 or Fax 44-71-779-8689).

- *Latin Finance* is a must for investors who are interested in Latin American privatization opportunities. Twice a year, *Latin Finance* publishes a special privatization supplement. The address for inquiries is *Latin Finance*, 2121 Ponce de Leon Blvd., Coral Gables, FL 33134 (Phone 305-448-6593 or Fax 305-448-0718).

The *Financial Times* of London also gives good coverage on current privatization developments, particularly in Europe. The *Financial Times* is now widely available in the United States.

PROFESSIONAL ADVICE

Most investors seek the assistance of professional advisers at some stage of their privatization project. Accountancy firms, particularly the Big Six,[1] tend to be the dominant providers of privatization advisory services. Investment banks are also an important source of advice. Additional, specialized advice may be sought from lawyers and consultants in such areas as market research, strategy, and manufacturing.

Areas in which such outside advisers typically are called on to play a role include:

---

[1] The "Big Six" include, in addition to Ernst & Young, KPMG Peat Marwick, Coopers & Lybrand, Arthur Andersen, Price Waterhouse, and Deloitte Touche Tohmatsu.

- *Identification and recommendation of potential investment targets.* The big accountancy firms, with their worldwide networks of offices, and, to a lesser extent, the major investment banks, provide an excellent listening post for gathering investment leads. The local partners and senior professionals have excellent contacts in the government and business community. They often hear of companies or activities that are to be privatized well before any public announcement is made. In some cases, the same accountancy firm may have been called upon to audit the SOE's books in the past and thus has a good idea of its financial and operational health.

- *Laying the groundwork for a possible acquisition.* The procedures and requirements for investing in an SOE vary from country to country, as does the cast of characters. Depending on the country and the specific deal in question, it may be necessary to visit different stakeholders (such as local governments and labor representatives), to explain the project, and learn as much as possible about the conditions under which they will support the investment project. An adviser who knows the local political and business environment can provide you with a road map to the privatization process, including obligatory meetings, and can help keep the discussions from being derailed.

- *Feasibility and due diligence analysis.* Advisers frequently are engaged to participate or to take the lead in assessing the proposed investment because (1) they have access to specialized knowledge and expertise (e.g., markets, technology, facilities), (2) the prospective investor does not have the staff resources to perform the study in-house, and/or (3) the adviser brings a new, objective point of view to the subject.

- *Financial analysis and evaluation.* Particularly in the post-Socialist countries, the structure of most SOEs' financial statements is so different from Western models that a specialist usually is required to interpret them meaningfully for the investor. In addition to their worldwide experience in privatization, the big accountancy firms have local offices whose professionals are fully conversant with local accounting conventions and can seek clarifications from SOE accountants when necessary. Valuation likewise is a highly specialized discipline, as well as one that calls for complete objectivity on the part of the valuer.

- *Environmental audit.* Because contingent liabilities can be such an explosive problem, the investor wants to be absolutely sure that he or she is aware of all the environmental issues that need to be dealt with in negotiations.

- *Preparing the investment proposal for submission to the seller.* The help of a knowledgeable adviser can be invaluable, not only in meeting all of the technical requirements of the law governing such proposals, but also in ensuring that the proposal addresses all relevant issues in a way that maximizes its chance of acceptance.

- *Advice on negotiating strategy.* A successful negotiating strategy has many elements: offering price, terms, representations and warranties requested from the government, and so forth. In addition to the actual terms of the agreement, the success of the negotiations can turn on cultural and personal factors as subtle as the turn of a particular phrase. Smart investors usually will want the advice of someone close to the deal, who is familiar with the real issues in the negotiations, to help them avoid any land mines and bring the deal to a successful closing.

- *Help in arranging financing.* Investors may want help in financing their share of the investment or in bringing other investors in to spread the risk around.

- *Coordinating the role of the other advisers.* Particularly in larger projects, the investor may appoint a lead adviser to coordinate the work of the various other specialists (e.g., legal, technical, marketing).

- *Postprivatization assistance.* Newly privatized SOEs usually require a certain amount of restructuring to integrate them with the owners' other business(es) and to realize their inherent competitive advantages. Management information systems, cost accounting, productivity measurement, and production management are just a few of the areas in which many former SOEs require strengthening. The new owners may call in consultants to assist them with the restructuring, just as they would in the parent company. However, the arguments in favor of using a consultant as opposed to in-house resources are somewhat stronger in the case of a former SOE, due to the distances and differences in business culture involved.

In reality, there is a lot of overlap among the types of advisory services provided by accountancy firms, investment banks, lawyers, and other consultants. The major accountancy firms, particularly Ernst & Young and the other Big Six, have evolved into integrated professional services firms that derive a large share of their revenues from activities not directly related to their audit business, such as valuations, mergers and acquisitions, and organizational improvement assistance (e.g., productivity improvement, quality control, management information systems).

Investment banks still have a near monopoly on arranging the largest (say over US$100 million) investment transactions, and lawyers obviously predominate where interpreting the law or fine-tuning offers to comply with the law are concerned, but otherwise the choice of adviser(s) should reflect the investor's preference and the qualifications and business terms offered by the adviser.

FINANCIAL ASSISTANCE FOR PROSPECTIVE INVESTORS

Financial assistance is available from various U.S. government and international agencies, under certain conditions, for the following purposes:

- To help defray certain preinvestment costs associated with performing a feasibility study and negotiating a deal
- To obtain project financing
- To insure the investment against political risk

Preinvestment costs, such as feasibility study costs, may be eligible for partial reimbursement under the U.S. Overseas Private Investment Corporation's (OPIC) Project Development Program. Through this program, which at present is limited to investments in Central and Eastern Europe and the former Soviet Union, OPIC will fund 50 percent (75 percent for small business) of the costs (up to $150,000) of conducting preinvestment analyses to determine the commercial viability of proposed investments. Should an investment project proceed based on the preliminary efforts funded by OPIC, the investor is expected to pay OPIC a "success fee" equal to the amount of the grant. Inquiries may be addressed to Overseas Private Investment Corp., Project Development Program, 1615 M Street, NW, Washington, DC 20527. (Phone 202-457-7011 or Fax 202-223-3514).

In the fall of 1993, OPIC reportedly was considering expanding this program to other regions, such as Africa and Asia. If you are looking at investment opportunities, in SOEs located in these regions, you may wish to check with OPIC in order to get an update on whether such preinvestment assistance is available for those regions.

Under certain circumstances, the U.S. Trade and Development Agency (TDA) provides nonreimbursable grants for U.S. companies to carry out preinvestment studies of major investment projects. Although most TDA undertakings have historically been public sector projects, the agency now considers funding for private sector projects as well, including joint ventures in which U.S. companies plan to take equity.

The formal request for TDA assistance should come from the appropriate government agency in the country that is selling the SOE, rather than the investor. You should have the privatization agency or other responsible organization prepare an official letter of request for forwarding to TDA in Washington, DC, containing a description of the proposed project and the required study. TDA's address is U.S. Trade and Development Administration, SA-16, Room 309, Washington, DC 20523 (Phone 703-875-4357 or Fax 703-875-4009).

TDA reviews the proposal to see if it meets TDA criteria. If it does, TDA signs an agreement with the appropriate government agency, which contracts with the U.S. firm to carry out the study or consultancy.

Project financing may be available from a number of U.S. government and international agencies. The main sources include

- OPIC
- The International Finance Corporation (part of the World Bank)

- The European Bank for Reconstruction and Development

- Inter-American Investment Corp. (part of the Inter-American Development Bank)

OPIC provides project financing assistance to U.S. investors meeting certain criteria, through direct loans and guarantees and political risk insurance. OPIC's loan guaranties cover both commercial and political risks. Guaranties are issued to U.S. lending institutions on behalf of eligible U.S. investors and typically range from $2 million to $50 million. OPIC's direct loans, reserved for small- and medium-sized companies, typically range from $500,000 to $6 million. OPIC will participate in up to 50 percent of the total project cost for a new venture and up to 75 percent of the total cost of an expansion.

OPIC insures eligible U.S. investors against two types of political risks: political violence and expropriation without fair compensation. OPIC insurance coverage extends to parent company equity and debt investments, institutional loans, leases, technical assistance rights and property as well as contractors' exposure in connection with bid and performance bonds, custom bonds, equipment, and other risks. For further information on OPIC project finance assistance, contact OPIC's Office of Investor Services at the address given earlier.

The International Finance Corporation (IFC), a member of the World Bank Group, is the largest source of direct project financing for private investment in developing countries. IFC invests in commercial enterprises of varying industries by means of loans and equity financing in collaboration with other investors. The loans and equity investments that IFC makes for its own account are usually limited to 25 percent of project cost, with the largest amount invested at around $100 million. For more information, contact International Finance Corporation, 1818 H Street NW, Washington, DC 20433 (Phone 202-477-1234).

The European Bank for Reconstruction and Development (EBRD) was formed three years ago to finance investments as well as to invest directly in projects in Central and Eastern Europe and the former Soviet Union. EBRD's portfolio of investment assistance services includes loans and equity investments, as well as guarantees and underwriting. Loans are normally denominated in convertible currencies or currency units, and EBRD does not normally accept currency risk on repayment. EBRD's loans to commercial enterprises, including those to SOEs undergoing privatization, are made without government guarantees and require a full commercial return that reflects the risks attached to them. EBRD limits its financing to 35 percent of the total cost of a borrower's total capital on a pro forma market value basis. EBRD does not make loans or investments for amounts under about $5 million. Additional information can be obtained from the European Bank for Reconstruction and Development, 122 Leaden Hall, London EC3V 4QL, United Kingdom (Phone 011-44-71-338-6424 or Fax 011-44-71-338-6100).

The Inter-American Investment Corp. functions much like the IFC but focuses its investment activities on the countries of Latin America. For additional information, contact Inter-American Investment Corp., Inter-American Development Bank, 1300 New York Ave. NW, Washington, DC 20577.

APPENDIX A SAMPLE PRIVATIZATION SALES CONTRACT

THIS AGREEMENT is made and entered into by and between _____ (hereinafter referred to as "the Seller" which term or expression as herein used shall as and where the context so requires or admits mean and include the said _____ aforesaid and his successors in the said Office for the time being and the persons who, for the time being, are acting in the Office of, or are performing the functions now exercised by, the Secretary to the Treasury) acting herein for and on behalf of the Government of _____ (hereinafter referred to as "the Government") of the one part and _____ (hereinafter referred to as "the Purchasers" which term or expression as herein used shall as and where the context so requires or admits mean and include the said _____ of the OTHER-PART.

WHEREAS the purchases are interested in engaging in industrial and commercial activities in the said

_____.

AND WHEREAS _____ Company Limited (hereinafter referred to as the "Company") is a Company duly incorporated in the said _____ under the Companies Act No. 17 of 1982, in terms of the conversion of Public Corporations or Government Owned Business Undertakings into Public Companies Act No. 23 of 1987.

AND WHEREAS the present issued Share Capital of the Company is One Hundred Million (—100,000,000/-) divided into 10,000,000 Ordinary Shares of —10/- each and are all held by the Seller for and on behalf of the Government.

AND WHEREAS consequent to the policy of the Government on privatization of state owned enterprises, it has been agreed between the parties hereto that the Purchasers shall purchase 9,000,000 (90%) Ordinary Shares of —10/- each (hereinafter referred to as the "Shareholding") out of the total shares held by the Seller for a sum of United States Dollars Forty One Million One Hundred Thousand (US$41,100,000) of lawful money of United States of America (hereinafter referred to as the "Purchase Consideration").

WHEREAS it has been further agreed between the parties hereto that the terms and conditions upon which the Purchasers shall purchase the said Shareholding, should be embodied in a Memorandum of Understanding (hereinafter referred to as the "Agreement").

NOW THIS AGREEMENT WITNESSETH as follows:

1. The Purchasers shall pay to the seller, the purchase Consideration of United States Dollars Forty One Million One Hundred Thousand (US$41,100,000) at the time of the execution of these presents as follows:

   a) A sum of United States Dollars Twenty Two Million Five Hundred Thousand (US$22.5 Mn) in United States Dollars (US$)

   b) The balance sum of United States Dollars Eighteen Million Six Hundred Thousand (US$18.6 Mn) in Lawful money of _____ converted at the rate prevailing on the date of executing this Agreement.

2. Upon the receipt of the United States Dollars Forty One Million One Hundred Thousand (US$ 41,100,000) as aforesaid being the Purchase Consideration on execution of these presents, the Seller shall deliver to the Purchasers a duly executed Instrument of Transfer in respect of the said Shareholding of the Company accompanied with the respective Share Certificates and shall ensure that such Shares be free from all options, claims, liens, charges, encumbrances and any other adverse interests.

3. The Seller hereby assures the Purchasers that no tax, levy or fee, other than the stamp duty payable on transfer of shares shall be payable by the Purchasers in respect of or in connection with or arising from the purchase of the said Shares by the Purchasers.

4. After receiving the prior approval of the Seller/Government which approval shall not be unreasonably withheld, the Purchasers will be entitled to sell in or outside _____ any or all Shares of the Company which the Purchasers may from time to time acquire.

5. The Purchasers agree to continue the employment of employees and staff on terms not less favourable than those at present applicable. The Purchasers shall not take any steps to retrench any employee of the Company from the date of the acquisition of the shares, provided however, this clause shall not affect in any way action taken by the Company on disciplinary grounds concerning its employees.

6. The Purchasers agree that all payments including compensation which are being made by the Company to employees/ex-employees of the Company or their next of kin and their dependents and arising from subversive/terrorist activity will continue to be paid by the Company in accordance with Public Administration Circular No. 21/88 and Government decisions/circulars regarding such payments.

7. The Purchasers agree to compute on the basis approved by the Seller, the share entitlement of the employees of the Company for the 10% of shares constituting 1,000,000 Ordinary Shares of —10/- each which is to be gifted to the employees out of the shares held by the Seller and forward to the Seller a list of such share entitlements within a month of acquiring the shares. The Purchasers agree to facilitate and execute the distribution of such shares immediately upon the approval of the said list by the seller.

8. The purchasers shall have had, before the date of execution of these presents entered into a technical collaboration agreement with regard to the rehabilitation of the company, with _____ and submitted a copy of same to the seller.

9. The purchasers shall have had forwarded to the seller a combined statement of the financial position of the

_____ to satisfy the Government prior to the date of execution.

10. The purchasers shall have had forwarded a certified copy of the certificate of Registration of _____ prior to the execution of these presents.

11. After the acquisition of Shares by the Purchasers, the Company should not enter into any Management or Technical agreement, without obtaining in writing the prior approval of the Seller which approval shall not be unreasonably withheld.

12. The Seller/Government shall ensure that the Company shall not until the transfer of the Management of the Company

   i.   Issue any Shares nor pay any dividend in cash or in kind on existing Shares without the prior consent of the Purchasers;

   ii. Buy or otherwise acquire sell or otherwise dispose of any substantial assets and make any payment or undertake any obligation which may materially affect the Financial Status of the Company and take any action which may materially affect the future performance of the Company without the prior consent of the Purchasers;

   iii. Employ any more employees of the Company or enhance the present employees teams and conditions of the employment;

OR

   iv. Terminate or enter into any agreements material to the operations of the Company.

13. The Seller and the Purchasers consent that this Agreement contain the entire understanding between the parties hereto in relation to the sale and purchase of the Shareholding of the Company and that there are no representations, promises, terms, conditions, warranties, undertakings, obligations, oral or written, expressed or implied other than

those contained herein which form part of or form the
basis of the Agreement between the parties hereto in
relation to such sale and purchase.

14. This Agreement shall be governed by and construed in
accordance with the laws of the said _____
and each party irrevocably agrees that the courts of the
said _____ shall have a jurisdiction to hear
and determine any suit, action or proceeding and to settle
any dispute which may arise out of or in connection with
this Agreement and for such purpose irrevocably, submits
to the exclusive jurisdiction of such courts.

IN WITNESS WHEREOF the said _____ as
Secretary to the Treasury aforesaid, acting herein for and on
behalf of the Government of _____ has set his
hand and Mr. _____ acting herein for and on behalf of
the said _____ Group of Companies have set his
hand hereto and to another of the same tenor and date as
these presents at _____ on this day of
_____ One Thousand Nine Hundred and Ninety Three.

. . . .
Secretary to the Treasury
for and on behalf of the
Government of _____

_____

Mr. . . . .
for and on behalf of
_____ Group of Companies.

APPENDIX B SAMPLE PRIVATIZATION SALES CONTRACT

AGREEMENT dated the   day of   1993

PARTIES

1.   His Majesty's Government of _____

2.   [   ] ("the Purchaser")

3.   [   ] ("the Guarantor")

INTRODUCTION

A.   _____ owns or controls 100% of the Shares ("Shares") in _____ Limited a Company registered under the Company Act 1964.

B.   _____ has agreed to sell and the Purchaser has agreed to purchase the Shares on the terms and conditions contained in this agreement.

C.   The Guarantor has agreed to guarantee the obligations of the Purchaser under this agreement.

AGREEMENT

I.   INTERPRETATION

1.1 In this agreement, unless the context otherwise requires:

"Advisors" means _____.

"Completion" means completion of the sale and purchase of the Shares in accordance with clause 5.2 or, as the context may require, the point in time at which such completion takes place.

"Completion Date" means _____ 1993 or such other date as the Vendor and the Purchaser may agree.

1.2   In this agreement, unless the context otherwise requires:

a)   Words importing one gender include the other gender;

b)   The singular includes the plural and vice versa;

c)   References to a month or a year are references to a calendar month or year, as the case may be.

1.3   In this agreement:

(a)   A reference to the _____, the Guarantor or the Purchaser is a reference also to their respective executors, administrators or successors.

(b)   A reference to a "person" includes an individual, firm, company, corporation or unincorporated body of persons, or any state or government or any agency thereof (in each case, whether or not having separate legal personality) and a reference in a "company" includes a person.

(c)   Headings are for convenience only and shall not affect interpretation;

(d)   References to sections, clauses and schedules are references to sections, clauses and schedules of this agreement unless specifically stated otherwise.

2.   SALE AND PURCHASE OF THE SHARES

2.1   _____ agrees to sell and the Purchaser agrees to purchase the Shares at the price specified, and upon the other terms and conditions in this agreement.

3.   PURCHASE PRICE

3.1   The purchase price for the Shares shall be an aggregate amount of _____

4.   PAYMENT

4.1 The Purchaser shall pay the purchase price for the Shares
     in the following manner:

     (a) By a deposit of [   ] upon the execution of this
         Agreement.

     (b) The balance of the purchase price shall be paid in
         cash on the Completion Date.

4.2 If from any cause whatever (excluding the default of
     HMGN under, or failure by the _____ to comply
     with, any provision of this agreement) any portion of the
     purchase price for the Shares is not paid on the due date,
     the Purchaser shall pay to _____ interest and
     surcharge at the rate of 25% per annum on the portion of
     the purchase price so unpaid, such interest to be payable
     from the due date for payment until actual payment
     thereof but this stipulation is without prejudice to any of
     _____ rights or remedies under this agreement.

5.   COMPLETION

5.1 Completion of the sale and purchase of the Shares shall
     take place not later than 12 noon on the Completion Date
     at the offices of the Ministry of Finance, _____.

5.2 At Completion;

     (a) Title to the Shares and possession of the Shares shall
         be given by _____ and _____
         accepted by the Purchaser;

     (b) shall ensure that the Directors of _____ shall
         resign.

     (c) _____ shall deliver to the Purchaser:

         (i) A memorandum of transfer of the Shares;

         (ii) All other documents and things reasonably
              necessary to transfer to the Purchaser full and

unencumbered title to and possession of the Shares.

All such documents referred to in clauses 5.2 (c) (i) and (ii) to be prepared by the Purchaser and submitted to the Vendor in sufficient time prior to the Completion Date to enable execution by _____.

(d) The Purchaser shall pay or satisfy the purchase price for the Shares in the manner specified in clause 4.1.

6.   INFORMATION ETC

6.1   In the period prior to Completion, _____ and _____ shall provide the Purchaser and its duly authorized representatives with access during the _____'s normal operating hours to the Business Records and the Business Premises to enable the Purchaser to familiarize itself with the affairs of the Company.

7.   WARRANTIES AND UNDERTAKINGS

7.1   In consideration of the Purchaser entering into this agreement, _____ warrants that the Shares are not now, nor will on Completion be subject to any option, mortgage, charge, lien, encumbrance, security interest or other adverse interest of any nature whatsoever.

7.2   The Purchaser acknowledges that it is entering into this agreement, and agreeing to purchase the Shares pursuant to this agreement, solely in reliance on its own judgment and inspection of the _____ Business and assets and not in reliance on any statements, warranties or representations made to the Purchaser or to any other person by or on behalf of _____ and, save for clause 7.1, all express or implied or other representations and warranties are hereby expressly excluded to the maximum extent permitted by law without limiting the foregoing, the Purchaser, acknowledges that save as to expressed in clause 7.1):

(a) none of _____, the Advisors, _____
or any person on behalf of any of them has made, or
is making, any representation or warranty, express or
implied, as to the accuracy or completeness of, or
otherwise in relation to, the Evaluation Material;

(b) none of _____, the Advisors, _____
or any person on behalf of any of them has given, or
will give, any representation or warranty as to the
future prospects of the business of _____;

(c) none of _____, the Advisors, _____
or any of their respective officers; directors,
employees, shareholders, affiliates or agents has any
liability to the Purchaser, or to any other person,
resulting from the use of any Evaluation Material by
the Purchaser;

(d) neither the provision of any Evaluation Material, nor
the entry by the Vendor into this agreement
constitutes any representation, warranty or
undertaking (express or implied) that the Evaluation
Material was or is correct or that there has been no
change in the business, affairs or financial state of
_____ either before or after the date of the
provision of the Evaluation Material to the Purchaser
or its agents or advisors;

(e) the Purchaser has made its own enquiries and
satisfied itself (after taking all such independent
advice as it has considered necessary or desirable) as
to all matters which are relevant (whether material
or not) to its decision to enter into, and perform its
obligations under, this agreement.

For the purpose of this clause 7.3 the expression
"Evaluation Material" means all information (whether
written or oral and held in any medium) statements,
projections, records, valuations, appraisals, forecasts,
estimates and opinions relating directly to the business
and the assets of _____ or the employees of the
Business and provided by _____ or any
department of _____, the Advisors, _____

or any of their respective officers, directors, employees, shareholders, affiliates, agents or advisors.

8.   EMPLOYEES

8.1   The Purchaser shall ensure that _____ shall continue to employ such of the employees of the Vendor as are engaged in _____ on the Completion Date as desire to continue employment with _____ on terms and conditions no less favorable (including terms relating to provident fund, leave compensation and gratuity) than those at present enjoyed by such employees, but subject to the provisions of clause 8.2.

8.2   (Notes

1.   This clause will contain provisions relating to entitlements of employees who remain in the employment of _____.

2.   The specific entitlements will be negotiated with the successful bidder and inserted in the final agreement.

3.   _____'s present intention is that redundancy costs will be met by _____, that _____ will accept responsibility for agreeing any redundancy package with employees and that _____ will retain liability for payment to employees of accrued gratuity and leave compensation at Completion Date).

9.   RIGHTS OF VENDOR

9.1   If the Purchaser defaults in the performance of any of its obligations under this agreement then _____ may, after giving to the Purchaser 3 days' notice in writing of such default requiring the Purchaser to remedy the same and such default not having been remedied within that period, exercise all or any of the following, without prejudice to any other rights, powers, authorities or remedies which the Vendor may have:

a) Cancel this agreement and in that event any moneys paid by way of deposit or installments of purchase price shall be absolutely forfeited to the Vendor;

b) Re-sell the Shares either by public auction or private contract for cash or on credit, and upon such other terms and conditions as _____ may think proper, with power to vary any contract for sale, buy in at any acution and resell, and any deficiency in price which may result and all expenses in attending a resale or attempted resale shall be made good by the Purchaser and shall be recoverable by _____ as liquidated damages, the Purchaser receiving credit for any payments made in reduction of the purchase price but any increase in price on resale after deduction of expenses belonging to _____;

c) Sue the Purchaser for specific performance.

10. ANNOUNCEMENTS

10.1 Except as may be required by law the Purchaser shall not make any announcements or disclosures as to the subject matter or any of the terms of this agreement except in such form and manner, and at such time, as may be approved by _____.

11. NOTICES

11.1 If any party wishes to give to or serve on another party any notice, claim, demand or other communication (a "notice") under or in connection with this agreement, the notice shall be sufficiently given or served (but without prejudice to any other mode of service) if addressed to that party and delivered to the address of that party stated below.

The Vendor and: _____

The Purchaser and the Guarantor:

12. **NO WAIVER**

12.1 No waiver of any breach, or failure to enforce any
provision, of this agreement at any time by any party
shall in any way affect, limit or waive the right of such
party thereafter to enforce and compel strict compliance
with the provisions of this agreement.

13. **COSTS**

13.1 The parties shall each bear their own costs and expenses
incurred in connection with the preparation and
implementation of this agreement. Any fees taxes or
stamp duty payable of transfer of the shares shall be
borne by the purchaser.

14. **GUARANTEE**

14.1 The Guarantor unconditionally and irrevocably guarantees
to _____ the due and punctual payment by the
Purchaser of all moneys from time to time payable by the
Purchaser under this agreement and the due, punctual and
proper performance and observance by the Purchaser of
all its other obligations under this agreement.

14.2 The liability of the Guarantor under this guarantee shall
constitute a principal obligation of the Guarantor and
such liability shall not be relieved or in any way affected
in a manner prejudicial to _____ by any granting
of time, waiver or forbearance to sue by _____ or
by any other act, omission, matter, circumstance or law
whereby the Guarantor as a surety only would but for the
provisions of this clause have been released from liability
hereunder.

15. **GOVERNING LAW**

15.1 This agreement shall be governed by, and construed in
accordance with, the laws of _____.

15.2 The Purchaser submits to the non-exclusive jurisdiction of the courts of _____ in respect of all matters arising out of this agreement.

<u>EXECUTION BY THE PARTIES</u>

Signed for and on behalf of _____

_____
      (Name)   (Position)

Signed by or on behalf of the Purchaser _____

_____
      (Name)   (Position)

Signed by the Guarantor in the presence of _____

_____
Signature of Witness

_____
Occupation

_____
Address

APPENDIX C ORGANIZATIONS TO CONTACT ABOUT PRIVATIZATION OPPORTUNITIES

ALBANIA
National Privatization
  Agency
Ministry of Finance
Tirana
Fax 356-42-28373

ARGENTINA
Privatization Secretary
Ministry of Economy
Palacio de Hacienda
Sala 819
Buenos Aires
Tel. 54-1-331-6423

AUSTRALIA
Treasure
The Treasury
Parkes Place
Parkes
ACT 2600
Tel. 61-6-263-2111

AUSTRIA
Finance Minister
Ministry of Fi ance
Himmelpfort Gasse
428 1010 Vienna
Tel. 43-1-514330

AZERBAIJAN
State Property Committee

Council of Ministers Office
Baku

BELARUS
Committee for
  Administration of State
  Property
U1. Mjasnikovs 39
220097 Minsk
Tel. 7-0172-270642
Fax 7-0172-296335

BOLIVIA
Unidad Ejecutora del
  Reordenamiento de la
  Empresa Publica
Ministerio de Hacienda y
  Desarollo
Piso 20
Edificio Centro de
  Comunicaciones
Avenida Mariscal Santa
  Cruz
La Paz
Tel. 591-2-357692
Fax 591-2-350526

BRAZIL
Finance Minister
Ministry of Finance
Explanada de Ministerios
Brasilia DF 7000

Tel. 55-61-226-1397
Fax 55-61-226-2499

BULGARIA
National Privatization
  Agency
29 Aksakov St.
1000 Sofia
Tel. 359-2-88-93-42
Fax 359-2-88-56-78

CANADA
Assistant Deputy Minister
  (Privatization)
Minto Place
6th Floor
Enterprise Building
427 Lautier Avenue W.
Ottowa
Ontario
K1A 1J2

CHILE
Corfo
Monada 921
Santiago
Tel. 56-2-638-0521
Fax 56-2-671-1058

CHINA
China Securities
  Supervision and
  Administration
  Committee

14 Dangzhimen Street
  South
Beijing 100027
Tel. 86-1-501-1291

COLOMBIA
Minister of Finance
Carrera 7
A6/45
Bogota
Tel. 57-1-286-1400
Fax 57-1-281-6381

COTE D'IVOIRE
Privatization Committee
Prime Minister's Office
01 BP 1141
Abidjan 01
Tel. 225-22-22-81
Fax 225-22-22-35

CROATIA
Agency for Privatization
  and Restructuring
Gajeva 20
Zagreb
Tel. 38-41-469-112
Fax 38-41-469-136

CZECH REPUBLIC
Ministry of Privatization
Zborovska 11
150 00 Prague 5
Tel. 42-2-213-0111
Fax 42-2-540-338

DENMARK
Ministry of Finance
Christiansborg Slotsplads 1
1218 Copenhagen
Tel. 45-3392-3333
Fax 45-3316-0127

ECUADOR
National Council for
  Modernization of the
  State
Juan Leon Mera 130 y Av.
  Patria
Edificio de la Corporacion
  Financiera Nacional
Quito
Tel. 593-2-509-432
Fax 593-2-509-437

EGYPT
Public Enterprise Office
2 Sharia Latin America
Cairo
Tel. 20-2-355-9253
Fax 20-2-355-9233

ESTONIA
Office of the Prime
  Minister
State Chancery
Talinn
Fax 7-014-440-372

FINLAND
Ministry of Trade and
  Industry
Alexsanterinkatu 10
00170 Helsinki
Tel. 358-0-160-3596
Fax 358-0-160-3598

FRANCE
Ministry of Economy
139 Rue de Bercy
75572 Paris
Cedex 12
Tel. 33-1-4004-0404

GEORGIA
State Property Committee
Havchavadze Street 64
Tbilisi
Tel. 7-883-2-222-294
Fax 7-883-2-983-083

GERMANY
Treuhandanstalt
Detlev-Rohwedder-Haus
Leipzigerstr., 5–7
0-1080, Berlin
Tel. 49-30-31540
Fax 49-30-31541036

GREECE
Economy Ministry
Syntagma Square
10180 Athens
Tel. 30-1-333-2631

Fax 30-1-323-9139
or
Industry Ministry
80 Michalakopoulou
11528 Athens
Tel. 30-1-771-4328
Fax 30-1-770-8595

GUYANA
Minister of Finance
Georgetown, Guyana
Fax 592-2-63395

HUNGARY
State Property Agency
Vigado Utca 6
1051 Budapest
Tel. 36-1-111-0200
Fax 36-1-118-4974

INDONESIA
Minister of Finance
J1 Lapangam Bantang
  Timur
No. 2–4 Jakarta Pusai
Tel. 62-21-385-384

IRELAND
Minister for Finance
Government Buildings
Merrion Street
Dublin 2
Tel. 353-1-767571

ISRAEL
Government Companies
  Authority
Ministry of Finance
1 Kaplan Street
Kiryat Ben-Gurion
POB 883
Jerusalem
Tel. 972-2-317446
Fax 972-2-617025

ITALY
Treasury Ministry
97 Via XX Setiembre
00187 Rome
Tel. 39-6-47611

JAMAICA
Director of Privatization
National Investment Bank
  of Jamaica
9th Floor
Scotia Center
Corner Duke and Port
  Royal Sts.
POB 889
Kingston
Tel. 1-809-92-20915
Fax 1-809-92-22282

JAPAN
Ministry of Finance
3-1-7 Kasumigaseki
Chiyoda-ku

Tokyo 100
Tel. 81-33-581-4111

KAZAKHSTAN
State Property Committee
Ablay Khan Ave. 93–95
480091 Almaty
Tel. 7-327-620453

KENYA
Privatization Committee
Nairobi
Fax 254-2-216796

KYRGYZSTAN
State Property Committee
720040 Erkindik 57
Bishkek
Tel. 7-833-12-227706
Fax 7-833-12-267004

LATVIA
Directorate of Large
  Company Privatizations
Ministry of Economic
  Reforms
Blvd. Brivibas 36
226170 Riga
Fax 7-0132-746089

LITHUANIA
Deputy Minister of
  Economics for
  Privatization
Gedimino pr 38/2

Vilnius
Fax 3702-623974

MALAYSIA
Privatization Task Force
Economic Planning Unit
Prime Minister's
  Department
Jalan Dato' Onn
50502 Kuala Lumpur
Tel. 60-3-230-0133
Fax 60-3-291-4268

MEXICO
Disincorporation Unit
Ministry of Finance
Palacio Nacional
4th Floor
06060 Mexico DF
Tel. 52-5-510-1994
Fax 52-5-542-2685

MOROCCO
Ministere des Affaires
  Economiques et de la
  Privatisation
Rabat
Tel. 212-7-61485
Fax 212-7-774776

NETHERLANDS
Commission for
  Privatization and
  Incorporation
Ministry of Finance

Casuariestraal 32
261 1 VB
The Hague
Tel. 3170-342-8000

NEW ZEALAND
Minister for State-Owned
  Enterprises
1 The Terrace
Wellington
Tel. 64-4-472-2733
Fax 64-4-479-0982

NIGERIA
Technical Committee for
  Privatization and
  Commercialization
POB 60238
Ikoyi
Lagos
Tel. 234-1-603660-5
Fax 234-1-685846

PAKISTAN
Privatization Commission
Ministry of Finance
EAC Building
5-A Constitution Ave.
Islamabad
Tel. 92-51-817-276
Fax 92-51-822-102

PERU
Copri
Av. Las Artes 260

San Borja
Lima
Tel. 51-14-756253
Fax 51-14-750078

PHILIPPINES
Technical Committee on
  Privatization
Central Bank 5-Storey
  Building
Mabini St.
Manila
Tel. 63-2-59-58-86
Fax 63-2-59-58-86

POLAND
Ministry of Privatization
ul. Mysia 5
Warsaw
Tel. 48-22-292010

PORTUGAL
Secretary of State for
  Privatization
Ministry of Finance
Avenide Inf. d. Henriques
Lisbon 1200
Tel. 351-1-878733

ROMANIA
National Agency for
  Privatization
Ministerului St.
Bucharest

Tel. 40-1-614-9495
Fax 40-1-912-0609

RUSSIA
Commission for the
  Administration of State
  Property
Proyezd Vladimirova d.9
Kom. 308
Moscow 103685
Tel. 7-095-298-7562
Fax 7-095-92408794

SINGAPORE
Ministry of Finance
8 Shenton Way
Treasury Building
0106 Singapore
Tel. 65-225-9911
Fax 65-920-9435

SLOVENIA
Agency for Privatization
Dunajska 104
POB 92
61109 Ljubljana
Tel. 38-61-112-122
Fax 38-61-118-011

SRI LANKA
Commercialization Division
Ministry of Finance
Galle Face Secretariat
Colombo 1

Tel. 94-1-33937, ext. 301
Fax 94-1-449823

THAILAND
National Economic and
  Social Development
  Board
962 Krung Kasem Road
Bangkok 10100
Tel. 66-2-281-1012
Fax 66-2-280-0892

TUNISIA
General Director of Public
  Enterprise
Prime Ministry
Le Kasbah
Tunis
Tel. 216-1-260072
Fax 216-1-567227

TURKEY
Public Participation
  Administration
Ataturk Bulvari
Bakanuktar
Ankara
Tel. 90-4-117-2611

UKRAINE
State Property Fund
3, Sadovaya St.
252008 Kiev
Tel. 7-044-226-26-11

UNITED KINGDOM
Financial Secretary
HM Treasury
Parliament St.
London SW1P3AG
Tel. 44-71-270-3000

UZBEKISTAN
Privatization Committee
Alley Paradov 6
Tashkent
Tel. 7-398-203-398083
Fax 7-371-2-398639

VENEZUELA
Fondo de Inversiones de
  Venezuela

Torre Financiera
Banco Central de
  Venezuela
Piso 20
Av. Urdaneta
Esq. Carmillitas
Caracas 1010
Tel. 58-2-832044
Fax 58-2-819324

VIETNAM
Ministry of Finance
8 Phan Huy Cho
Hanoi
Fax 84-42-62-266

Annotated Bibliography

Asian Development Bank. Privatization. *Policy, Methods and Procedures*. Manila: Asian Development Bank, 1985.

This book includes a summary of the proceedings at a Conference on Privatization Policies, Methods and Procedures sponsored by the Asian Development Bank, as well as the compiled papers presented at the conference.

Blake, Thomas M. and Michael S. Blake. "Bear Necessities," *Global Competitor*, Winter 1994.

The article describes the authors' first-hand experience in negotiating business deals in post-Socialist Russia. Although relatively brief, the article contains interesting insights into the challenges facing prospective foreign investors in newly privatized state enterprises.

Butler, Stuart, et al. *Privatizacion, Una Alternativa Para El Desarrollo*. Bogotá: Camara de Comercio de Bogotá, 1989.

This publication in Spanish looks at the economic and political fundamentals of models of privatization. It discusses a global perspective on privatization as well as techniques and strategies.

El-Naggar, Said. *Privatization and Structural Adjustment in Arab Countries*. International Monetary Fund. 1989.

This volume focuses on privatization efforts in the Middle Eastern countries of Jordan, Tunisia, and Egypt. It includes information on opportunities for financial market development and case studies on the role of the public and private sectors in privatization.

Ellerman, David P. *Management & Employee Buy-Outs as a Technique of Privatization.* Central and Eastern European Privatization Network, 1993.

This book is the third volume of the Workshop Series published by the Central and Eastern European Privatization Network (CEEPN). It presents the results of the October 1992 conference in Ljubljana, Slovenia on Management and Employee Buy-Outs (MEBO's) as a Technique of Privatization.

Erdmann, Peter B. *Columbia Journal of World Business, Focus Issue: Privatization.* Spring 1993.

This focus issue on privatization includes eighteen articles on privatization programs worldwide. This issue includes case studies in Eastern Europe and Latin America as well as analyses of programs in Asia and Africa.

Goldman, Harvey and Sandra Mokuvos. *The Privatization Book.* New York: Arthur Young, 1984.

This book is a "how to" guide for privatization. It presents a complete explanation of the basics combining privatization theory and implementation. Discussions include financing and legal issues, state and federal roles, and public/private partnership formation.

Hanke, Steve H. *Privatization & Development.* San Francisco: International Center for Economic Growth, 1987.

This book discusses theoretical and practical aspects of privatization in the developing world. It is a compilation of leading privatization experts' works demonstrating the privatization process and progress.

Hanke, Steve H. *Prospects for Privatization.* New York: The Academy of Political Science, 1987.

This book overviews privatization efforts in specific industries including urban buses, airports, and waterworks around the world.

Kikeri, Sunita; John Nellis and Mary Shirley. *Privatization, The Lessons of Experience*. Washington, D.C.: The World Bank, 1992.

This World Bank publication provides information on privatization strategy and implementation including history of past reform efforts and the impact of such efforts. Implementation methods addressed include pricing and valuation, financing, and managing privatization.

Lord, Rodney. *Privatisation Yearbook*. London: Privatisation International, 1993.

This yearbook outlines issues such as the political and economic background, main elements of privatization strategies, and opportunities for western investors for over fifty countries.

Mohnot, Dr. S.R. *Privatization, Options and Challenges*. New Dehli: Center for Industrial and Econornic Research, 1991.

This volume looks at international experience with privatization and the debate over privatization. It presents the technical papers from an international conference put on by the Center for Industrial and Economic Research. It includes several case studies in the power sector, the steel industry, and the agricultural sector.

Ramamurti, Ravi and Raymond Vernon. *Privatization and Control of State-Owned Enterprises*. EDI Developme The World Bank, 1991.

This volume provides analysis of privatization and performance contracting for policy makers and practitioners charged with improving the performance of state-owned enterprises. It includes three case studies. This publication is a companion to another volume in the EDI Development Studies series, Public Enterprise Reform: The Lessons of Experience *by Mary Shirley and John Nellis.*

Roth, Gabriel. *The Private Provision of Public Services in Developing Countries*. Washington, D.C.: The World Bank, 1987.

Part of the EDI Series in Economic Development, this book explores the roles between the public and the private sectors. It concentrates on cases in which private delivery systems have demonstrated advantages over publicly provided alternatives.

Qureshi, Moeen A. *Reflections on Development.* Washington D.C., World Bank. 1991.

This is compilation of articles on issues facing developing countries. It includes a section on the future of private enterprise in developing countries, risks of foreign investment, and opportunities for investors.

Vuylsteke, Charles. *Techniques of Privatization of State Owned Enterprises.* Washington, D.C.: The World Bank, 1988.

This volume reviews recent experience in selected developing countries. It examines methods tried and the results of implementation. This book is one of a series of three volumes. The other two volumes are Selected Country Case Studies, *and* Inventory of Country Experience and Reference Materials.

NEWSLETTERS

Many of the books exploring the privatization process tend to be academic in nature. The following two publications may provide more practical and up-to-date information on privatization programs and opportunities world-wide, for those interested in pursuing investment via privatization.

Privatisation International. London.

This monthly publication provides up-to-date reports on privatization and project financing worldwide. For subscription information write to:

> Privatisation International Ltd
> Suite 510
> Butlers Wharf Business Centre
> 45 Curlew Street
> London, SE1 2ND, UK

Telephone: (+44 71) 378 1620
Fax: (+44 71) 403 7876

The International Privatization Update. New York.

This monthly review provides an outlook for professionals involved in privatization. For subscription information write to:

Financial Market Research, Inc.
P.O. Box 33
Castleton-on-Hudson, New York 12033

Telephone: (518) 732-5756

Glossary of Privatization-Related Terms

Asset valuation: An approach to estimating the fair market value of a state-owned enterprise or assets which is based on the replacement value of the assets, adjusted for physical, functional, and economic depreciation. (See also **Fair market value; Valuation.**)

Auction: A privatization technique in which an SOE or its assets are sold to the highest offer or in open bidding.

BOT or BOOT (Build(-Own)-Operate-and-Transfer) agreement: An approach to privatization that is used mainly for infrastructure projects. The private investor pays the cost of constructing a toll road, bridge, or the facility, then is entitled to collect a share of the revenues for an agreed period (say, 20 years), after which ownership and/or revenues revert to the government.

Business valuation: An approach to estimating the fair market value of a state-owned enterprise which is based on the discounted value of the future cash flows the enterprise is expected to generate. (See also **Fair market value; Valuation.**)

Commercialization: Commercialization is often the first step on the road to privatization, by making the management of a state enterprise responsible for the company's financial results and terminating government operating subsidies.

Company risk: Investment risks that are specific to a particular company, such as the danger that it will lose a key customer and that it will not be able to find alternative markets. (See also **Country risk.**)

Compensation: The practice of paying the former private owner(s) of a state enterprise or property which was taken over by the government in cash or other financial instruments instead of returning the assets themselves.

Concession: An approach to privatization in which the private investor pays either a fixed fee or a percentage of his profits for the right to operate a facility or provide a service, keeping the rest of the proceeds.

Contracting out: See **Management contract.**

Core investor: A private investor which takes a controlling interest in a former state enterprise and participates actively in the management of the company.

Corporatization: The process whereby a state enterprise is transformed into a shareholding company preparatory to privatization.

Country risk: Investment-related risks that are common to all companies in a particular country, such as inflation or civil unrest. (See also **Company risk.**)

Coupon privatization: Eligible citizens are given or sold (at a nominal price) coupons or vouchers, which can be exchanged for shares in former state-owned companies or in investment funds which invest directly company shares. (See also **Investment fund; Mass privatization.**)

Debt-equity swap: Some countries permit private investors to finance their investment in a state enterprise by buying up the country's foreign debt in secondary markets at a discount, then redeeming it at face value in payment for the investment.

Due diligence: Prior to making an investment, prudent investors or their advisors perform a "due diligence" review of the offering memorandum and other data and documentation on the enterprise in question, to determine the accuracy of the data and the reasonableness of the assumptions made, such as future sales projections.

Enabling environment: All of the policy, legal, institutional, financial, infrastructural, and other elements which are prerequisites of a functioning market economy, and without which private investments (including investments in privatizing SOEs) in these countries have a high probability of failure.

ESOP (Employee share ownership plan):   In an ESOP, employees of an SOE undergoing privatization are given the opportunity to purchase shares in the company, often at a discount or on favorable terms.

Fair market value: The value at which a state enterprise would change hands between a willing buyer and a willing seller, neither of whom is under compulsion to sell.

Going concern: A state enterprise which is sold as a going concern is sold as a functioning business, e.g., together with employees and intangible assets such as the company name and customer relationships. The alternative to sale as a going concern is liquidation of the enterprise.

Golden share: Where the government wishes to retain a voice in the management of a state enterprise which is being privatized, but creation of a mixed public–private enterprise is deemed inadvisable, the government can achieve similar objectives through an agreement (the "golden share") which guarantees it a vote or the right to be consulted on certain issues, without an actual ownership share.

Greenfield investment: Investing in the start-up of a new facility or business, instead of investing in an existing (state-owned) one.

Investment fund: In the context of "mass privatization" (see entry below), a mutual fund is a state- or privately-organized entity which is set up to manage the investment of investors' privatization vouchers or coupons in former state-owned companies.

ISTEA (Intermodal Surface Transporation Efficiency Act):   An act of the US Congress which allows states to levy tolls on existing and new Federally aided bridges, roads, and tunnels. ISTEA should facilitate privately financed infrastructure schemes such as BOOT (Build-Own-Operate-Transfer) projects.

Joint venture: Joint ventures can be viewed as either a type of privatization or an alternative to it, in which the private investor and the SOE join forces to form a distinct legal entity, but one which preserves the distinction between public and private capital.

Leasing: A limited form of privatization, in which the private investor pays the government an agreed annual fee to operate an SOE or other publicly owned facility (which remains state property), but is entitled to keep the balance of the operating profits.

Liquidation: An approach to privatization in which an SOE's business is terminated and its assets sold.

Management contract: An alternative to outright privatization of a state enterprise or public service, whereby the government retains ownership but pays a contractor an agreed fee to operate it.

Management/employee buyout: A type of privatization where the management and/or employees of a state enterprise buy a controlling interest in the company.

Market valuation: A technique of estimating the fair market value of a state-owned enterprise or assets based on comparable transactions elsewhere.

Mass privatization: A technique of privatization, pioneered in Eastern Europe, which involves the distribution (free or for a nominal fee) of shares in state companies to eligible members of the population, such as all adult citizens. (See also **Coupon privatization; Investment funds; Voucher privatization.**)

MBO: Management buy-out (See also **Management/ employee buyout.**)

Mixed enterprise: An enterprise in which the government retains partial ownership following privatization.

MLE: Medium/large enterprise. The actual criteria (e.g., employment, annual turnover) used to distinguish MLEs from small enterprises may vary from country to country. In any case, its chief significance lies in the techniques which generally are used to privatize MLEs: tenders, negotiated sales, mass privatization. (See entries for each of these terms.) Small enterprises such as shops, service establishments, and trucks, on the other hand, are usually sold at auction.

Mutual fund: See **Investment fund.**

Negotiated sale: A type of privatization transaction in which the price and terms of the transaction are agreed in direct negotiations between the buyer and seller.

Portfolio investor: An investor who purchases a share in an SOE in the expectation of financial returns, but who does not take an active role in managing the enterprise.

Privatization: The transfer or sale of any asset, organization, function, or activity from the public to the private sector. As such, in addition to the sale of publicly owned assets the term privatization also may be applied to joint public–private ventures, concessions, leases, management contracts, as well as some specialized instruments such as build-own-operate-and transfer (BOOT) agreements.

Restitution: Restoring a state enterprise or property to former private owners whose title was assumed by the state.

Restructuring: All the actions undertaken by enterprise management or government to bridge the gap between the current performance of an enterprise, group of enterprises or sector, to bring current performance up to internationally competitive levels. (In the context of privatization, there has been considerable debate over the extent to which an attempt should be made to restructure state enterprises in order to make them more attractive to private buyers.)

Self-privatization: The enterprise initiates its own privatization, with or without government approval. In Hungary, for instance, state enterprises are permitted to initiate privatization proceedings, subject only to the government's final approval.

Small privatization: Small privatization refers to the privatization of retail shops, service establishments, trucks, and similar assets, usually at auction.

SOE: State-owned enterprise.

Spontaneous privatization: The process occurring, particularly in Russia and other former Soviet republics, whereby management is assuming control of state enterprises' management and finances without government approval. The term "spontaneous privatization" is also used formally in Hungary to describe a type of privatization in which the state enterprise transforms itself into a shareholding company, but the transaction is carried out largely by the State Property Agency.

Stakeholder: Any individual or group whose interests are affected by a proposed privatization, including, but not necessarily limited to: managers, employees, suppliers, customers, creditors, government officials, politicians, etc.)

Stock flotation: A privatization technique in which the government's shares in an SOE are offered on local or international capital markets.

Stock distribution: A feature of some governments' privatization strategies whereby a percentage of shares (generally in the 10–25 percent range) in SOEs are given or sold at preferential terms to employees and in some cases, other special groups.

Strategic investor: See **Core investor.**

Transparency: A "transparent" privatization process is one which is conductd openly and according to clearly defined rules, in order to minimize the possibility of misconduct.

Tender: A privatization technique in which bidders submit sealed bids which are opened at an announced time, with the property generally going to the highest bidder.

Valuation: Estimating the fair market value of a state-owned enterprise or assets to be privatized (See also **Asset valuation; Business valuation; Fair market value; Market valuation.**)

Voucher privatization: See **Coupon privatization.**

Index